The Angular Mini-Book

Matt Raible

Version 3.0.1 | 2023-08-29

The Angular Mini-Book

Published by C4Media, publisher of InfoQ.com.

Production Editor: Ana Ciobotaru
Copy Editor: Maureen Spencer
Technical Editor: Alisa Duncan and Deepu K Sasidharan
Cover and Illustrations: David Neal

Library of Congress Cataloguing-in-Publication Data:
ISBN: 978-1-312-35074-8

Table of Contents

Dedication

I dedicate this book to my partner, Trish McGinity. She's taught me to love, laugh, and opt outside more. Since I met her in 2010, I've rekindled my relationship with the great outdoors via whitewater rafting, mountain biking, and skiing.

Trish, your sweet smile and giddyup attitude make me want to raft, ride, and ski with you as often as possible.

I love you, sweetheart!

Acknowledgments

I'm incredibly grateful to Trish, Abbie, and Jack. They put up with my late nights and extended screen time while I worked on this book.

To Miško Hevery, thank you for inventing Angular and changing the lives of front-end developers. To the whole Angular team, I appreciate you and all you do for the community. Kudos for making our apps faster with every release!

Thanks to Phil Webb and Dave Syer for creating Spring Boot and simplifying Java for everyone. Hats off to the whole Spring team for their tireless dedication to quality open source projects.

I want to thank this book's tech editors, Alisa Duncan and Deepu K Sasidharan. I looked to them for their deep experience with Angular, TypeScript, and JavaScript. Many sections are more streamlined because of their advice.

This book's copy editor, Maureen Spencer, helped correct my grammar and make this book easier on the eyes. I'm thankful for your help, Maureen.

Finally, my compliments to you, dear reader. It's a heckuva time to be writing code. Enjoy your learning adventures!

Preface

I've been developing websites and web applications since the 1990s. Along the way, I've become a web framework aficionado. I appreciate web frameworks because of their patterns, their testability, and the flourishing communities that tend to sprout around them.

I started working with open source web frameworks, notably Struts and Spring MVC, in the early 2000s. I spent a few years developing with them (mainly doing server-side MVC), then returned to UI development with HTML, JavaScript, and CSS. Boy, did I have good timing!

The JavaScript Renaissance started in the mid-2000s with jQuery. jQuery leveled the playing field to write code that would work on most popular browsers and freed developers from the browser wars burden. From there, full-fledged JavaScript frameworks like Ember.js, Backbone.js, and AngularJS took the developer world by storm.

Java didn't have much innovation while the JavaScript Renaissance was happening. I was a Java developer at LinkedIn from 2007-2008, then moved to full-time front-end development with GWT and jQuery at Evite in 2009. The front-end landscape flourished for the next few years while the Java ecosystem languished.

In 2009, Node.js was created as well as the first version of npm. Node allows you to run JavaScript outside a browser, and JavaScript found itself well-positioned on the server.

In 2013, GitHub created Electron and introduced a way to write multi-platform desktop applications with JavaScript. Some of the most often-used software that developers use today (Slack and VS Code) are powered by Electron!

In 2014++, along came React, Angular (with TypeScript), and Vue. They continue to be the dominant frameworks for writing browser-based applications.

Another notable release happened in 2014: Spring Boot 1.0. Spring Boot was a breath of fresh air for those using the Spring framework with its starters and simplified configuration. Spring Boot led to Spring Cloud, and both helped fuel the microservices boom that continues today.

I wanted to write this book because Angular and Spring Boot are among the most powerful combinations for writing web apps today. You can use JHipster to generate an app with both frameworks, but if you want to learn how something works, it's essential to know the building blocks.

What is in an InfoQ mini-book?

InfoQ mini-books are concise, intending to serve technical architects looking to get a firm conceptual understanding of new technology or techniques in a quick yet in-depth fashion. These books cover a topic strategically or essentially. After reading a mini-book, the reader should have a fundamental understanding of the technology, including when and where to apply it, how it relates to other technologies, and an overall feeling that they have assimilated the combined knowledge of other professionals who have already figured out what this technology is about. The reader will then be able to make intelligent decisions about the technology, once their projects require it, and can delve into sources of more detailed information (such as larger books or tutorials) at that time.

Who is this book for?

This book is aimed specifically at web or Java developers who want a rapid introduction to Angular, Bootstrap, and Spring Boot.

What do you need for this book?

To try code samples in this book, you will need a computer running an up-to-date operating system (Windows, Linux, or Mac OS X). You will need Node.js and Java installed. The book code was tested against Node.js v14 and JDK 11, but newer versions should also work.

Conventions

We use several typographical conventions within this book that distinguish between different kinds of information.

Code in the text, including commands, variables, file names, CSS class names, and property names, are shown as follows:

> The Angular CLI will create a ng-demo project and run npm install in it.

A block of code is set out as follows. It may be colored, depending on the reader format you're using.

Listing 1. src/app/search/search.component.html

```
<form>
  <input type="search" name="query" [(ngModel)]="query"
(keyup.enter)="search()">
  <button type="button" (click)="search()">Search</button>
</form>
```

Listing 2. src/app/search/search.component.ts

```
export class SearchComponent implements OnInit {
  query: string | undefined;
  searchResults: any;

  constructor() { }

  ngOnInit(): void { }

  search(): void { }

}
```

When we want to draw your attention to certain lines of code, those lines are annotated using numbers accompanied by brief descriptions.

```
export class SearchComponent {
  constructor(private searchService: SearchService) {} ①

  search(): void { ②
    this.searchService.search(this.query).subscribe( ③
      data => { this.searchResults = data; },
      error => console.log(error)
    );
  }
}
```

① To inject `SearchService` into `SearchComponent`, add it as a parameter to the constructors' argument list.

② `search()` is a method that's called from the HTML's `<button>`, wired up using the `(click)` event handler.

③ `this.query` is a variable that's wired to `<input>` using two-way binding with `[(ngModel)]="query"`.

Tips are shown using callouts like this.

 Warnings are shown using callouts like this.

Sidebar

Additional information about a certain topic may be displayed in a sidebar like this.

Finally, this text shows what a quote looks like:

> In the end, it's not the years in your life that count. It's the life in your years.

— Abraham Lincoln

Reader feedback

We always welcome feedback from our readers. Tell us what you thought about this book—what you liked or disliked. Reader feedback helps us develop titles that deliver the most value to you.

To send us feedback, e-mail us at feedback@infoq.com, send a tweet to @mraible, or post a question on Stack Overflow using the "angular" tag.

If you're interested in writing a mini-book for InfoQ, see http://www.infoq.com/minibook-guidelines.

The most up-to-date version of this book can be downloaded from https://infoq.com/minibooks/angular-mini-book.

Introduction

Angular is a web framework that helps you build web, mobile web, native mobile, and desktop applications. Angular apps are authored in TypeScript, compiled to JavaScript, and run in browser-based runtimes that have become fast and efficient over the last decade.

Like Struts in the early 2000s and Rails in the mid-2000s, Angular and other JavaScript frameworks have changed the way developers write applications. Today, data is exposed via REST APIs, and UIs are written in JavaScript (or TypeScript).

As a Java web developer, I was immediately attracted to AngularJS when I saw its separation of concerns: controllers, services, and directives for data manipulation. Then along came Angular 2.0 in 2016, and changed everything. The team adopted TypeScript as Angular's default language, refined its architecture for the future, and created awesome tools like the Angular CLI.

It worked! The Angular project is still going strong five years later.

The Angular team releases a major version every six months, often with backward compatibility, making for a thriving and enthusiastic open source community. Want to make your users happy? Just make it easy to upgrade!

An Angular app is composed of several building blocks:

- Components: Classes that retrieve data from services and expose it to templates.
- Services: Classes that make HTTP calls to an API.
- Templates: HTML pages that display data from components.
- Pipes: Data-transformation tools (e.g., format dates, currency, etc.).
- Directives: HTML processors that simplify logic in templates. Similar to JSP tags.

This book shows you how to build apps with Angular and guides you through many tools, techniques, security best practices, and production deployment options.

I hope you learn something from it!

PART
ONE

Build an Angular App

Before you start creating an Angular app, I think it's useful to know a bit about the history of Angular. Its first version was called AngularJS. Then, from its second version until today, it's been called Angular.

A Brief History of Angular

AngularJS was started by Miško Hevery in 2009. He was working on a project that was using GWT (Google Web Toolkit). Three developers had been developing the product for six months, and Miško rewrote the whole thing in AngularJS in three weeks. At that time, AngularJS was a side project he'd created. It didn't require you to write much in JavaScript, as you could program most of the logic in HTML. The GWT version of the product contained 17,000 lines of code. The AngularJS version was only 1,000 lines of code!

In October 2014, the AngularJS team announced they were building Angular 2.0. The announcement led to a bit of upheaval in the Angular developer community. The API for writing Angular applications would change, and it would be based on a new language, AtScript. There would be no migration path, and users would have to continue using 1.x or rewrite their applications for 2.x.

In March 2015, the Angular team addressed community concerns, announced they would be using TypeScript over AtScript and that they would provide a migration path for Angular 1.x users. They also adopted semantic versioning and recommended people call it "Angular" instead of Angular 2.0.

Angular 2.0 was released in September 2016. Angular 4.0 was released in March 2017. The Angular project releases two major versions each year to keep Angular synchronized with the rest of the JavaScript ecosystem and have a predictable schedule. They released Angular 15 on November 18, 2022.

You can find the Angular project at angular.io.

Developers like to see things working in minutes. I'm a developer, and I like to evaluate software with a "10-minute test." If I can get it working in 10 minutes, sign me up!

Rather than explain all the concepts in Angular, I'll show you how to build a basic application. You'll learn how to write unit tests, integration tests, add authentication, and deploy to production.

I should warn you about my teaching style. My words will tell you to do things that cause errors to happen. You'll think you did something wrong. However, if you return to my instructions, you'll find that error was expected. When you see errors happen, make sure to keep reading.

Prerequisites:

- A favorite text editor or IDE. I recommend IntelliJ IDEA [https://www.jetbrains.com/idea/].
- Node.js [http://nodejs.org/] and npm installed.
- Angular CLI [https://angular.io/cli] installed.

If you don't have the Angular CLI installed, please install it:

```
npm install -g @angular/cli@15
```

 IntelliJ IDEA Ultimate Edition has the best support for TypeScript. If you'd rather not pay for your IDE, check out Visual Studio Code [https://code.visualstudio.com/].

Create a new Angular project

Create a new project using the ng new command from Angular CLI:

```
ng new ng-demo
```

When prompted to install Angular routing, type "Y". For the stylesheet format, choose "CSS" (the default).

This will create a ng-demo project and run npm install in it. It takes about a minute to complete but will vary based on your internet connection speed.

You can see the version of Angular CLI you're using with the ng version command.

```
$ ng version
```

```
Angular CLI: 15.2.0
Node: 18.14.0
Package Manager: npm 9.3.1
OS: darwin arm64

Angular:
...

Package                          Version
------------------------------------------------------------
@angular-devkit/architect        0.1502.0 (cli-only)
@angular-devkit/core             15.2.0 (cli-only)
@angular-devkit/schematics       15.2.0 (cli-only)
@schematics/angular              15.2.0 (cli-only)
```

If you run this command from the ng-demo directory, you'll see even more information.

```
....

Angular: 15.2.0
... animations, cli, common, compiler, compiler-cli, core, forms
... platform-browser, platform-browser-dynamic, router

Package                          Version
------------------------------------------------------------
@angular-devkit/architect        0.1502.0
@angular-devkit/build-angular    15.2.0
@angular-devkit/core             15.2.0
@angular-devkit/schematics       15.2.0
@schematics/angular              15.2.0
rxjs                             7.8.0
typescript                       4.9.5
```

Run the application

The project is configured with a simple web server for development. To start it, run:

```
ng serve
```

You should see a screen like the one below at `http://localhost:4200`.

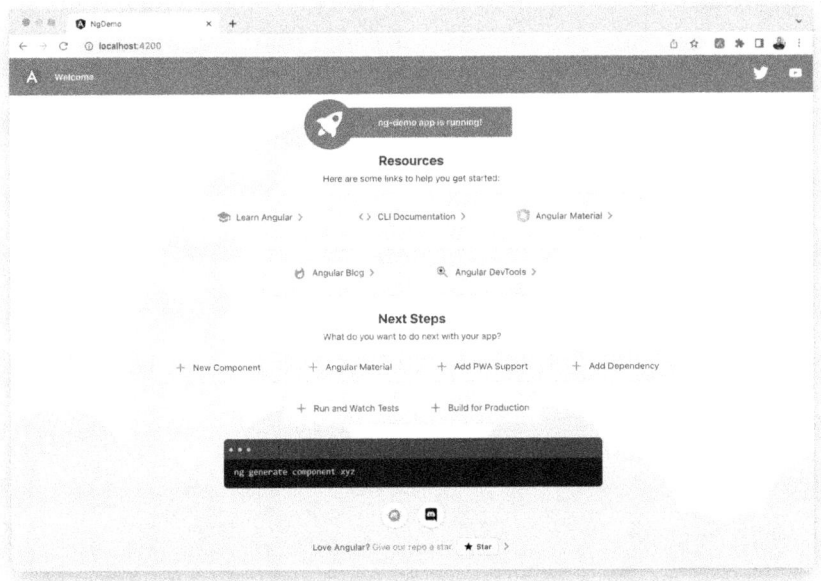

Figure 1. Default homepage

You can make sure your new project's tests pass, run `ng test`:

```
$ ng test
...
...: Executed 3 of 3 SUCCESS (0.061 secs / 0.055 secs)
```

Add a search feature

To add a search feature, open the project in an IDE or your favorite text editor.

In a terminal window, cd into your project's directory and run the following command to create a search component.

```
ng g component search
```

 `ng g` is an alias for `ng generate`.

Open `src/app/search/search.component.html` and replace its default HTML with the following:

Listing 3. src/app/search/search.component.html

```html
<h2>Search</h2>
<form>
  <input type="search" name="query" [(ngModel)]="query"
(keyup.enter)="search()">
  <button type="button" (click)="search()">Search</button>
</form>
<pre>{{searchResults | json}}</pre>
```

Add a query property to `src/app/search/search.component.ts`. While you're there, add a `searchResults` property and an empty `search()` method.

Listing 4. src/app/search/search.component.ts

```ts
export class SearchComponent implements OnInit {
  query: string | undefined;
  searchResults: any;

  constructor() { }

  ngOnInit(): void { }

  search(): void { }

}
```

In `src/app/app-routing.module.ts`, modify the `routes` constant to add `SearchComponent` as the default:

Listing 5. src/app/app-routing.module.ts

```ts
import { SearchComponent } from './search/search.component';

const routes: Routes = [
  { path: 'search', component: SearchComponent },
  { path: '', redirectTo: '/search', pathMatch: 'full' }
];
```

Run `ng serve` again you will see a compilation error.

```
ERROR in src/app/search/search.component.html:3:37 - error NG8002:
  Can't bind to 'ngModel' since it isn't a known property of 'input'.
```

To solve this, open `src/app/app.module.ts` and add `FormsModule` as an import in `@NgModule`:

Listing 6. src/app/app.module.ts

```
import { FormsModule } from '@angular/forms';

@NgModule({
  ...
  imports: [
    ...
    FormsModule
  ]
  ...
})
export class AppModule { }
```

Run `ng serve` again, and now you should be able to see the search form when you visit `http://localhost:4200/search`.

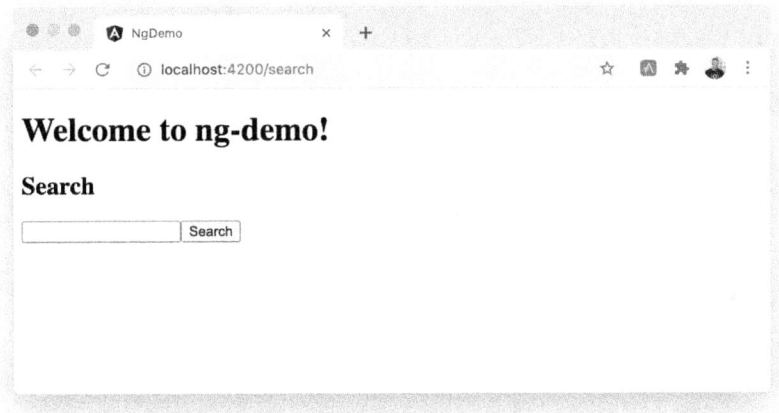

Figure 2. Search component

If yours looks different, it's because I trimmed my `app.component.html` to the bare minimum.

Listing 7. src/app/app.component.html

```
<h1>Welcome to {{ title }}!</h1>

<router-outlet></router-outlet>
```

If you want to add styling for this component, open `search.component.css` and add some CSS. For example:

Listing 8. src/app/search/search.component.css

```
:host {
  display: block;
  padding: 0 20px;
}
```

The `:host` allows you to target the container of the component. It's the only way to target the host element. You can't reach the host element inside the component with other selectors because it's not part of the component's template.

This section has shown you how to generate and add a new component to a basic Angular application with the Angular CLI. The next section shows you how to create and use a JSON file and `localStorage` to create a fake API.

The Back end

To get search results, create a `SearchService` that makes HTTP requests to a JSON file. Start by generating a new service.

```
ng g service shared/search/search
```

Create `src/assets/data/people.json` to hold your data.

```
mkdir -p src/assets/data
```

Listing 9. src/assets/data/people.json

```
[
  {
    "id": 1,
    "name": "Nikola Jokić",
    "phone": "(720) 555-1212",
    "address": {
      "street": "2000 16th Street",
      "city": "Denver",
      "state": "CO",
      "zip": "80202"
    }
  },
```

```
  {
    "id": 2,
    "name": "Jamal Murray",
    "phone": "(303) 321-8765",
    "address": {
      "street": "2654 Washington Street",
      "city": "Lakewood",
      "state": "CO",
      "zip": "80568"
    }
  },
  {
    "id": 3,
    "name": "Aaron Gordon",
    "phone": "(303) 323-1233",
    "address": {
      "street": "46 Creekside Way",
      "city": "Winter Park",
      "state": "CO",
      "zip": "80482"
    }
  }
]
```

Modify src/app/shared/search/search.service.ts and provide HttpClient as a dependency in its constructor.

In this same file, create a getAll() method to gather all the people. Also, define the Address and Person classes to which JSON will be marshaled.

Listing 10. src/app/shared/search/search.service.ts

```typescript
import { Injectable } from '@angular/core';
import { HttpClient } from '@angular/common/http';
import { Observable } from 'rxjs';

@Injectable({
  providedIn: 'root'
})
export class SearchService {

  constructor(private http: HttpClient) { }

  getAll(): Observable<Person[]> {
    return this.http.get<Person[]>('assets/data/people.json');
  }
}

export class Address {
  street: string;
  city: string;
```

```
    state: string;
    zip: string;

    constructor(address: Partial<Address> = {}) {
      this.street = address?.street || '';
      this.city = address?.city || '';
      this.state = address?.state || '';
      this.zip = address?.zip || '';
    }
  }

export class Person {
  id: number | null;
  name: string;
  phone: string;
  address: Address;

  constructor(person: Partial<Person> = {}) {
    this.id = person?.id || null;
    this.name = person?.name || '';
    this.phone = person?.phone || '';
    this.address = person?.address || new Address();
  }
}
```

To make these classes easier to consume by your components, create
src/app/shared/index.ts and add the following:

Listing 11. src/app/shared/index.ts

```
export * from './search/search.service';
```

The reason for creating this file is so you can import multiple classes on a
single line rather than having to import each class on separate lines.

In search.component.ts, add imports for these classes.

Listing 12. src/app/search/search.component.ts

```
import { Person, SearchService } from '../shared';
```

You can now add a proper type to the searchResults variable. While you're
there, modify the constructor to inject the SearchService.

Listing 13. src/app/search/search.component.ts

```
export class SearchComponent implements OnInit {
  query: string | undefined;
```

```
searchResults: Person[] = [];

constructor(private searchService: SearchService) { }
```

Then update the search() method to call the service's getAll() method.

Listing 14. src/app/search/search.component.ts

```
search(): void {
  this.searchService.getAll().subscribe({
    next: (data: Person[]) => {
      this.searchResults = data;
    },
    error: error => console.log(error)
  });
}
```

At this point, if your app is running, you'll see the following message in your browser's console.

```
NullInjectorError: No provider for HttpClient!
```

To fix the "No provider" error from above, update app.module.ts to import HttpClientModule.

Listing 15. src/app/app.module.ts

```
import { HttpClientModule } from '@angular/common/http';

@NgModule({
  ...
  imports: [
    ...
    HttpClientModule
  ],
  providers: [],
  bootstrap: [AppComponent]
})
```

Now clicking the search button should work. To make the results look better, remove the <pre> tag and replace it with a <table> in search.component.html.

Listing 16. src/app/search/search.component.html

```
<table *ngIf="searchResults?.length">
```

```
<thead>
<tr>
  <th>Name</th>
  <th>Phone</th>
  <th>Address</th>
</tr>
</thead>
<tbody>
<tr *ngFor="let person of searchResults; let i=index">
  <td>{{person.name}}</td>
  <td>{{person.phone}}</td>
  <td>{{person.address.street}}<br/>
    {{person.address.city}}, {{person.address.state}}
{{person.address.zip}}
  </td>
</tr>
</tbody>
</table>
```

What's up with *ngIf and ?.

You might be asking yourself why there's an asterisk in front of ngIf. From Angular's docs:

Angular transforms the asterisk in front of a structural directive into an <ng-template> that surrounds the host element and its descendants.

These two HTML snippets render the same output:

```
<p *ngIf="condition">
  Not all heroes wear capes!
</p>

<template [ngIf]="condition">
  <p>
    Not all heroes wear capes!
  </p>
</template>
```

As far as the ?. is concerned, that's how you do null-safe property traversal in TypeScript. It's officially called optional chaining and was introduced in TypeScript 3.7.

Then add some additional CSS to search.component.css to improve its table layout.

Listing 17. src/app/search/search.component.css

```
table {
  margin-top: 10px;
  border-collapse: collapse;
}

th {
  text-align: left;
  border-bottom: 2px solid #ddd;
  padding: 8px;
}

td {
  border-top: 1px solid #ddd;
  padding: 8px;
}
```

Now the search results look better.

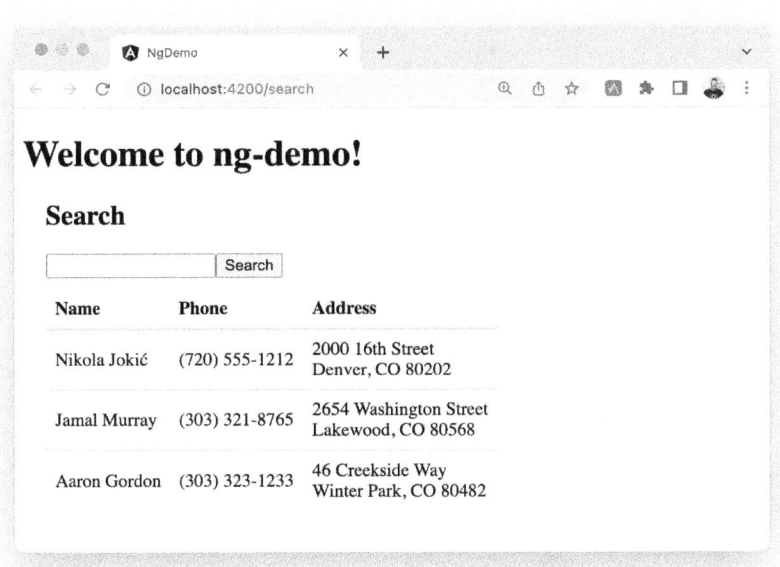

Figure 3. Search results

But wait, you still don't have search functionality! To add a search feature, add a search() method to SearchService.

Listing 18. src/app/shared/search/search.service.ts

```
import { map, Observable } from 'rxjs';
...

  search(q: string): Observable<Person[]> {
    if (!q || q === '*') {
      q = '';
    } else {
      q = q.toLowerCase();
    }
    return this.getAll().pipe(
      map((data: Person[]) => data
        .filter((item: Person) =>
JSON.stringify(item).toLowerCase().includes(q)))
    );
  }
```

Then refactor SearchComponent to call this method with its query variable.

Listing 19. src/app/search/search.component.ts

```
search(): void {
  this.searchService.search(this.query).subscribe({
    next: (data: Person[]) => {
      this.searchResults = data;
    },
    error: error => console.log(error)
  });
}
```

This won't compile right away.

```
Error: src/app/search/search.component.ts:18:31 - error TS2345:
 Argument of type 'string | undefined' is not assignable to parameter of type
'string'.
```

Since query will always be assigned (even if it's empty), change its variable declaration to:

```
query!: string; // query: string = ''; will also work
```

This is called a definite assignment assertion. It's a way to tell TypeScript, "I know what I'm doing; the variable will be assigned."

Now, the search results will be filtered by the query value you type in.

This section showed you how to fetch and display search results. The next section builds on this and shows how to edit and save a record.

Add an edit feature

Modify search.component.html to wrap the person's name with a link.

Listing 20. src/app/search/search.component.html

```
<td><a [routerLink]="['/edit', person.id]">{{person.name}}</a></td>
```

Run the following command to generate an EditComponent.

```
ng g component edit
```

Add a route for this component in app-routing.module.ts:

Listing 21. src/app/app-routing.module.ts

```
import { EditComponent } from './edit/edit.component';

const routes: Routes = [
  { path: 'search', component: SearchComponent },
  { path: 'edit/:id', component: EditComponent },
  { path: '', redirectTo: '/search', pathMatch: 'full' }
];
```

Update src/app/edit/edit.component.html to display an editable form. You might notice I've added id attributes to most elements. This is to make it easier to locate elements when writing integration tests.

Listing 22. src/app/edit/edit.component.html

```
<div *ngIf="person">
  <h3>{{person.name}}</h3>
  <div>
    <label>Id:</label>
    {{person.id}}
  </div>
  <div>
    <label>Name:</label>
    <input [(ngModel)]="person.name" name="name" id="name"
placeholder="Name"/>
  </div>
  <div>
    <label>Phone:</label>
```

```
        <input [(ngModel)]="person.phone" name="phone" id="phone"
placeholder="Phone"/>
    </div>
    <fieldset>
      <legend>Address:</legend>
      <address>
        <input [(ngModel)]="person.address.street" id="street"><br/>
        <input [(ngModel)]="person.address.city" id="city">,
        <input [(ngModel)]="person.address.state" id="state" size="2">
        <input [(ngModel)]="person.address.zip" id="zip" size="5">
      </address>
    </fieldset>
    <button (click)="save()" id="save">Save</button>
    <button (click)="cancel()" id="cancel">Cancel</button>
</div>
```

Modify EditComponent to import model and service classes and to use the
SearchService to get data.

Listing 23. src/app/edit/edit.component.ts

```
import { Component, OnInit, OnDestroy } from '@angular/core';
import { Person, SearchService } from '../shared';
import { Subscription } from 'rxjs';
import { ActivatedRoute, Router } from '@angular/router';

@Component({
  selector: 'app-edit',
  templateUrl: './edit.component.html',
  styleUrls: ['./edit.component.css']
})
export class EditComponent implements OnInit, OnDestroy {
  person!: Person;
  sub!: Subscription;

  constructor(private route: ActivatedRoute,
              private router: Router,
              private service: SearchService) {
  }

  async ngOnInit(): Promise<void> {
    const params = this.route.snapshot.params;
    const id = +params['id']; // (+) converts string 'id' to a number
    this.sub = this.service.get(id).subscribe(person => {
      if (person) {
        this.person = person;
      } else {
        this.gotoList();
      }
    });
  }
```

```
ngOnDestroy(): void {
  if (this.sub) {
    this.sub.unsubscribe();
  }
}

async cancel() {
  await this.router.navigate(['/search']);
}

async save() {
  this.service.save(this.person);
  await this.gotoList();
}

async gotoList() {
  if (this.person) {
    await this.router.navigate(['/search', {term: this.person.name}]);
  } else {
    await this.router.navigate(['/search']);
  }
}
}
```

Modify SearchService to contain functions for finding a person by their id and saving them. While you're in there, modify the search() method to be aware of updated objects in localStorage.

Listing 24. src/app/shared/search/search.service.ts

```
search(q: string): Observable<Person[]> {
  if (!q || q === '*') {
    q = '';
  } else {
    q = q.toLowerCase();
  }
  return this.getAll().pipe(
    map((data: Person[]) => data
      .map((item: Person) => !!localStorage['person' + item.id] ?
        JSON.parse(localStorage['person' + item.id]) : item)
      .filter((item: Person) =>
JSON.stringify(item).toLowerCase().includes(q))
    ));
}

get(id: number): Observable<Person> {
  return this.getAll().pipe(map((all: Person[]) => {
    if (localStorage['person' + id]) {
      return JSON.parse(localStorage['person' + id]);
    }
```

```
    return all.find((e: Person) => e.id === id);
  }));
}

save(person: Person) {
  localStorage['person' + person.id] = JSON.stringify(person);
}
```

You can add CSS to `src/app/edit/edit.component.css` to make the form look a bit better.

Listing 25. src/app/edit/edit.component.css

```
:host {
  display: block;
  padding: 0 20px;
}

button {
  margin-top: 10px;
}
```

At this point, you should be able to search for a person and update their information.

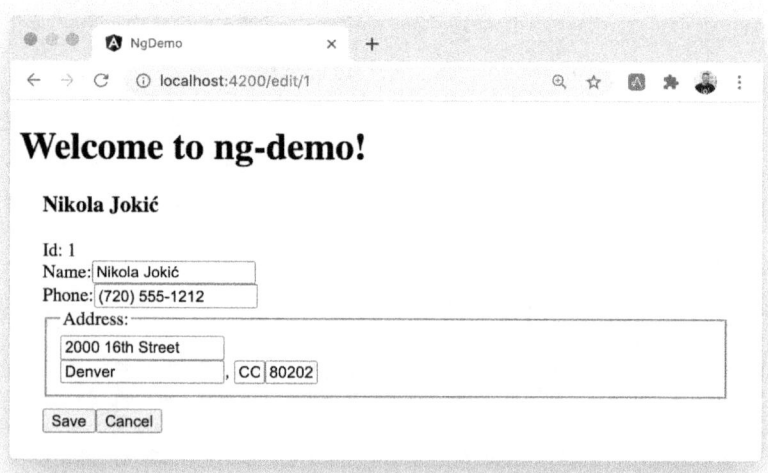

Figure 4. Edit component

The `<form>` in `src/app/edit/edit.component.html` calls a `save()` function to update a person's data. You already implemented this above. The function calls a gotoList() function that appends the person's name to the URL when sending the user back to the search screen.

Listing 26. src/app/edit/edit.component.ts

```
async gotoList() {
  if (this.person) {
    await this.router.navigate(['/search', {term: this.person.name}]);
  } else {
    await this.router.navigate(['/search']);
  }
}
```

Since the SearchComponent doesn't execute a search automatically when you execute this URL, add the following logic to do so in its ngOnInit() method.

Listing 27. src/app/search/search.component.ts

```
import { ActivatedRoute } from '@angular/router';
...

  constructor(private searchService: SearchService, private route:
ActivatedRoute) { }

  ngOnInit(): void {
    const params = this.route.snapshot.params;
    if (params['term']) {
      this.query = decodeURIComponent(params['term']);
      this.search();
    }
  }
```

After making all these changes, you should be able to search/edit/update a person's information. If it works—nice job!

Add Form Validation

You might notice that you can clear any input element in the form and save it. At the very least, the name field should be required. Otherwise, there's nothing to click on in the search results.

To make the name field required, modify edit.component.html to add a required attribute to the name <input> and bind it to Angular's validation with #name="ngModel". Add a <div> next to the field to display an error message when validation fails.

Listing 28. src/app/edit/edit.component.html

```
<input [(ngModel)]="person.name" name="name" id="name" placeholder="Name"
required #name="ngModel"/>
<div [hidden]="name.valid || name.pristine" style="color: red">
  Name is required
</div>
```

You'll also need to wrap everything in a <form> element. Add <form> after the <h3> tag and close it before the last </div>. You'll also need to add an (ngSubmit) handler to the form, give it the name of editForm, and change the save button to be a regular submit button that's disabled when the form is invalid.

Listing 29. src/app/edit/edit.component.html

```
<h3>{{person.name}}</h3>
<form (ngSubmit)="save()" #editForm="ngForm">
  ...
  <button type="submit" id="save"
[disabled]="!editForm.form.valid">Save</button>
  <button (click)="cancel()" id="cancel">Cancel</button>
</form>
```

After making these changes, the name field will be required.

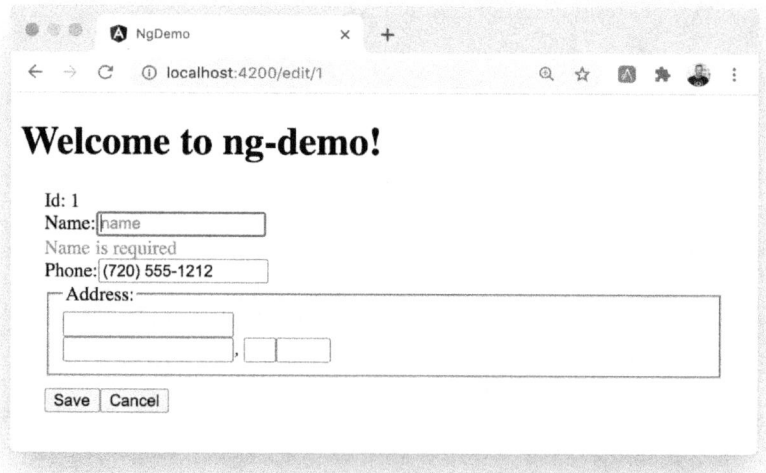

Figure 5. Edit form with validation

In this screenshot you might notice the address fields are blank, and the save button is enabled. The error in your console explains this.

```
If ngModel is used within a form tag, either the name attribute must be set
or the form control must be defined as 'standalone' in ngModelOptions.

Example 1: <input [(ngModel)]="person.firstName" name="first">
Example 2: <input [(ngModel)]="person.firstName"
[ngModelOptions]="{standalone: true}">
```

To fix this, add a name attribute to all the address fields. For example:

Listing 30. src/app/edit/edit.component.html

```
<address>
  <input [(ngModel)]="person.address.street" name="street" id="street"><br/>
  <input [(ngModel)]="person.address.city" name="city" id="city">,
  <input [(ngModel)]="person.address.state" name="state" id="state" size="2">
  <input [(ngModel)]="person.address.zip" name="zip" id="zip" size="5">
</address>
```

Now values display in all fields, name is required, and save is disabled when the form is invalid.

Figure 6. Edit form with names and validation

To learn more about forms and validation, see Angular's Validating form input documentation [https://angular.io/guide/form-validation].

Unit and End-to-End Testing

Now that you've built an application, it's important to test it to ensure it works. The best reason for writing tests is to automate your testing. Without tests, you'll likely be testing manually. This manual testing will take longer and longer as your application grows.

In this section, you'll learn to use Jasmine [http://jasmine.github.io/] for unit testing controllers and Cypress [https://www.cypress.io/] for integration testing.

Fix the Tests

If you run ng test, you'll likely get failures for the components and service you created. These failures will be solved as you complete the section below. The ng test command will start a process that listens for changes, so all you need to do is edit/save files, and tests will be automatically run again.

 You can use x and f prefixes before describe and it functions to *exclude* or *only* run a particular test.

Fix the AppComponent test

If you changed the app.component.html template as I did, you'll need to modify app.component.spec.ts to account for the change in HTML. Change its last test to look for an <h1> element and the welcome message inside it.

Listing 31. src/app/app.component.spec.ts

```
it('should render title', () => {
  const fixture = TestBed.createComponent(AppComponent);
  fixture.detectChanges();
  const compiled = fixture.nativeElement as HTMLElement;
  expect(compiled.querySelector('h1')?.textContent)
    .toContain('Welcome to ng-demo!');
});
```

Now this test should pass.

Unit test the SearchService

Modify search.service.spec.ts and set up the test's infrastructure (a.k.a. TestBed) using HttpClientTestingModule and HttpTestingController.

Listing 32. src/app/shared/search/search.service.spec.ts

```
import { TestBed } from '@angular/core/testing';
import { SearchService } from './search.service';
import { HttpClientTestingModule, HttpTestingController } from
'@angular/common/http/testing';

describe('SearchService', () => {
  let service: SearchService;
  let httpMock: HttpTestingController;

  beforeEach(async () => {
    await TestBed.configureTestingModule({
      imports: [HttpClientTestingModule],
      providers: [SearchService]
    });

    service = TestBed.inject(SearchService);
    httpMock = TestBed.inject(HttpTestingController);
  });

  it('should be created', () => {
    expect(service).toBeTruthy();
  });
});
```

Now, you will likely see some errors about the test stubs that Angular CLI created for you. You can ignore these for now.

```
NullInjectorError: R3InjectorError(DynamicTestModule)[SearchService -> HttpClient -> HttpClient]:
  NullInjectorError: No provider for HttpClient!

NullInjectorError: R3InjectorError(DynamicTestModule)[ActivatedRoute -> ActivatedRoute]:
  NullInjectorError: No provider for ActivatedRoute!
```

`HttpTestingController` allows you to mock requests and use its `flush()` method to provide response values. Since the HTTP request methods return an `Observable`, you can subscribe to it and create expectations in the callback methods. Add the first test of `getAll()` to `search.service.spec.ts`.

The test below should be on the same level as `beforeEach`. Passing the done function into the test ensures the test doesn't complete and exit before all the asserts are run.

Listing 33. src/app/shared/search/search.service.spec.ts

```
it('should retrieve all search results', (done) => {
  const mockResponse = [
```

```
    {name: 'Nikola Jokić'},
    {name: 'Mike Malone'}
  ];

  service.getAll().subscribe((people: any) => {
    expect(people.length).toBe(2);
    expect(people[0].name).toBe('Nikola Jokić');
    expect(people).toEqual(mockResponse);
    done();
  });

  const req = httpMock.expectOne('assets/data/people.json');
  expect(req.request.method).toBe('GET');
  req.flush(mockResponse);
});
```

While you're there, add an afterEach() to verify requests.

Listing 34. src/app/shared/search/search.service.spec.ts

```
afterEach(() => {
  httpMock.verify();
});
```

Add a couple more tests for filtering by search term and fetching by id.

Listing 35. src/app/shared/search/search.service.spec.ts

```
it('should filter by search term', (done) => {
  const mockResponse = [{name: 'Nikola Jokić'}];

  service.search('nik').subscribe((people: any) => {
    expect(people.length).toBe(1);
    expect(people[0].name).toBe('Nikola Jokić');
    done();
  });

  const req = httpMock.expectOne('assets/data/people.json');
  expect(req.request.method).toBe('GET');
  req.flush(mockResponse);
});

it('should fetch by id', (done) => {
  const mockResponse = [
    {id: 1, name: 'Nikola Jokić'},
    {id: 2, name: 'Mike Malone'}
  ];

  service.get(2).subscribe((person: any) => {
    expect(person.name).toBe('Mike Malone');
```

```
    done();
  });

  const req = httpMock.expectOne('assets/data/people.json');
  expect(req.request.method).toBe('GET');
  req.flush(mockResponse);
});
```

Unit test the SearchComponent

To unit test the SearchComponent, you can mock the methods in SearchService with spies [http://angular-tips.com/blog/2021/07/unit-testing-spies-and-mocks/]. These allow you to *spy* on functions to check if they were called.

You can use TestBed.configureTestingModule() to set up ActivatedRoute to have a specific parameter. In the second beforeEach(), you can see that the search() method is spied on, and its results are mocked. The response isn't important in this case because you're just unit testing the SearchComponent.

Listing 36. src/app/search/search.component.spec.ts

```
import { ComponentFixture, TestBed } from '@angular/core/testing';
import { SearchComponent } from './search.component';
import { SearchService } from '../shared';
import { ActivatedRoute } from '@angular/router';
import { RouterTestingModule } from '@angular/router/testing';
import { FormsModule } from '@angular/forms';
import { of } from 'rxjs';
import { HttpClientTestingModule } from '@angular/common/http/testing';

describe('SearchComponent', () => {
  let component: SearchComponent;
  let fixture: ComponentFixture<SearchComponent>;
  let mockSearchService: SearchService;

  beforeEach(async () => {
    await TestBed.configureTestingModule({
      declarations: [SearchComponent],
      providers: [
        {
          provide: ActivatedRoute,
          useValue: {
            snapshot: {
              params: {term: 'nikola'}
            }
          }
        }
      ],
      imports: [FormsModule, RouterTestingModule, HttpClientTestingModule]
```

```
    }).compileComponents();
  });

  beforeEach(() => {
    // mock response
    mockSearchService = TestBed.inject(SearchService);
    mockSearchService.search = jasmine.createSpy().and.returnValue(of([]));

    // initialize component
    fixture = TestBed.createComponent(SearchComponent);
    component = fixture.componentInstance;
    fixture.detectChanges();
  });

  it('should create', () => {
    expect(component).toBeTruthy();
  });
});
```

Add two tests, one to verify a search term is used when it's set on the component, and a second to verify search is called when a term is passed in as a route parameter.

Listing 37. src/app/search/search.component.spec.ts

```
it('should search when a term is set and search() is called', () => {
  component = fixture.componentInstance;
  component.query = 'J';
  component.search();
  expect(mockSearchService.search).toHaveBeenCalledWith('J');
});

it('should search automatically when a term is on the URL', () => {
  fixture.detectChanges();
  expect(mockSearchService.search).toHaveBeenCalledWith('nikola');
});
```

Update the test for EditComponent, verifying fetching a single record works. Notice how you can access the component directly with fixture.componentInstance, or its rendered version with fixture.nativeElement.

Listing 38. src/app/edit/edit.component.spec.ts

```
import { EditComponent } from './edit.component';
import { TestBed } from '@angular/core/testing';
import { Address, Person, SearchService } from '../shared';
import { ActivatedRoute } from '@angular/router';
import { FormsModule } from '@angular/forms';
```

```
import { of } from 'rxjs';
import { HttpClientTestingModule } from '@angular/common/http/testing';

describe('EditComponent', () => {
  let mockSearchService: SearchService;

  beforeEach(async () => {
    await TestBed.configureTestingModule({
      declarations: [EditComponent],
      providers: [
        {
          provide: ActivatedRoute,
          useValue: {
            snapshot: {
              params: {id: 1}
            }
          }
        }
      ],
      imports: [FormsModule, HttpClientTestingModule]
    }).compileComponents();

    mockSearchService = TestBed.inject(SearchService);
  });

  it('should fetch a single record', () => {
    const fixture = TestBed.createComponent(EditComponent);

    const person = new Person({id: 1, name: 'Michael Porter Jr.'});
    person.address = new Address({city: 'Denver'});

    // mock response
    spyOn(mockSearchService, 'get').and.returnValue(of(person));

    // initialize component
    fixture.detectChanges();

    // verify service was called
    expect(mockSearchService.get).toHaveBeenCalledWith(1);

    // verify data was set on component when initialized
    const editComponent = fixture.componentInstance;
    expect(editComponent.person.address.city).toBe('Denver');

    // verify HTML renders as expected
    const compiled = fixture.nativeElement;
    expect(compiled.querySelector('h3').innerHTML)
      .toBe('Michael Porter Jr.');
  });
});
```

You should see "`Executed 11 of 11 SUCCESS" in the shell window that's running ng test. If you don't, try canceling the command and restarting.

Integration test the search UI

To test if the application works end-to-end, you can write tests with Cypress [http://www.cypress.io/]. These are also known as integration tests since they test the *integration* between all application layers.

If you're an experienced Angular developer, you might be wondering, "What happened to Protractor?" Protractor support was removed in Angular 12 [https://github.com/angular/protractor/issues/5502], and other options such as Cypress, WebdriverIO, and TestCafe are being considered for future versions.

 If you're experienced with Protractor, see Migrating from Protractor to Cypress [https://docs.cypress.io/guides/migrating-to-cypress/protractor].

To add Cypress to your Angular project, you can use the official Cypress Angular Schematic [https://www.npmjs.com/package/@cypress/schematic].

```
ng add @cypress/schematic
```

When prompted to proceed and use Cypress for ng e2e, answer "Yes".

This will add Cypress as a dependency and create configuration files to work with Angular and TypeScript. Rename cypress/e2e/spec.cy.ts to home.cy.ts and change it to look for the title of your app.

Listing 39. cypress/e2e/home.spec.ts

```
describe('Home', () => {
  it('Visits the initial project page', () => {
    cy.visit('/')
    cy.contains('Welcome to ng-demo!')
    cy.contains('Search')
  })
})
```

Then, run ng e2e. This will compile your app, start it on http://localhost:4200, and launch the Cypress Electron app.

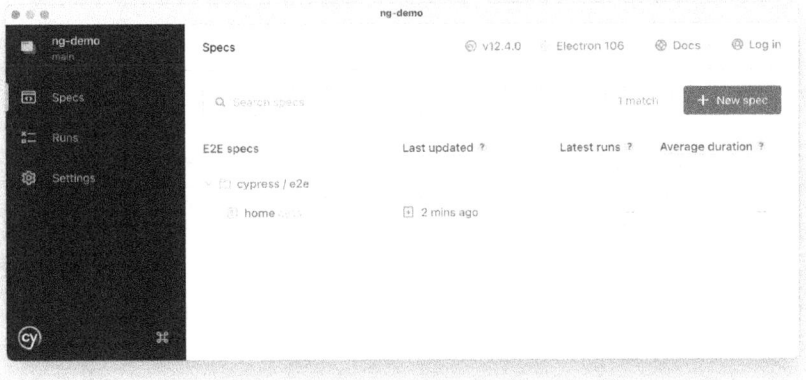

Figure 7. Cypress Electron App

If you click on the file name, it'll launch a browser and run the test. You can use this feature to step through your tests, find selectors for elements, and much more. You can learn more about Cypress' features at Setting up Cypress for an Angular Project [https://armno.in.th/2020/02/26/cypress-angular-integration-testing/].

I prefer the Protractor experience, where you could just run the command, it would run all the tests, and the user doesn't need to interact. You can do this with Cypress too!

The Cypress Angular Schematic added a few scripts to your `package.json`:

```
"scripts": {
  ...
  "e2e": "ng e2e",
  "cypress:open": "cypress open",
  "cypress:run": "cypress run"
}
```

To use the no-interaction approach, you'll need to start your app:

```
npm start
```

Then, run the Cypress tests for it in another window:

```
npm run cypress:run
```

 You might notice Cypress creates a video. You can disable

this by adding `video: false` to your `cypress.config.ts` file.

```
export default defineConfig({
  e2e: { ... },
  video: false,
  component: { ... }
})
```

The `npm run cypress:run` command will run a headless browser so that you won't see anything happening on your screen.

If you want to see the tests run, append `-- --browser chrome --headed` to the command. Add this to your `package.json` if you want to make it the default. See Cypress' launching browsers [https://docs.cypress.io/guides/guides/launching-browsers] documentation for a list of supported browsers.

You can also install concurrently [https://www.npmjs.com/package/concurrently] to run multiple tasks with one command.

```
npm install -D concurrently
```

Then, add a `cy:run` script to your `package.json`:

```
"scripts": {
  ...
  "cy:run": "concurrently \"ng serve\" \"cypress run\""
}
```

Then, you can run `npm run cy:run` to start your app and continuously run end-to-end tests on it when you change files.

Testing the search feature

Create another end-to-end test in `cypress/e2e/search.cy.ts` to verify the search feature works. Populate it with the following code:

Listing 40. cypress/e2e/search.cy.ts

```
describe('Search', () => {

  beforeEach(() => {
    cy.visit('/search')
  });
```

```
it('should have an input and search button', () => {
  cy.get('app-root app-search form input').should('exist');
  cy.get('app-root app-search form button').should('exist');
});

it('should allow searching', () => {
  cy.get('input').type('A');
  cy.get('button').click();
  const list = cy.get('app-search table tbody tr');
  list.should('have.length', 3);
});
});
```

Testing the edit feature

Create a `cypress/e2e/edit.cy.ts` test to verify the `EditComponent` renders a person's information and that their information can be updated.

Listing 41. cypress/e2e/edit.cy.ts

```
describe('Edit', () => {

  beforeEach(() => {
    cy.visit('/edit/1')
  });

  it('should allow viewing a person',  () => {
    cy.get('h3').should('have.text', 'Nikola Jokić');
    cy.get('#name').should('have.value', 'Nikola Jokić');
    cy.get('#street').should('have.value', '2000 16th Street');
    cy.get('#city').should('have.value', 'Denver');
  });

  it('should allow updating a name', () => {
    cy.get('#name').type(' Rocks!');
    cy.get('#save').click();
    // verify one element matched this change
    const list = cy.get('app-search table tbody tr');
    list.should('have.length', 1);
  });
});
```

With your app running, execute `npm run cypress:run` to verify all your end-to-end tests pass. You should see a success message similar to the one below in your terminal window.

```
(Run Finished)

   Spec                                    Tests  Passing  Failing  Pending  Skipped

 ✔ edit.spec.ts                    979ms     2        2        -        -        -

 ✔ home.spec.ts                    356ms     1        1        -        -        -

 ✔ search.spec.ts                  823ms     2        2        -        -        -

 ✔ All specs passed!               00:02     5        5        -        -        -
```

Figure 8. Cypress success

If you made it this far and have all your specs passing—congratulations! You're well on your way to writing quality code with Angular and verifying it works.

You can see the test coverage of your project by running `ng test --no-watch --code-coverage`.

You'll see a printout of code coverage in your terminal window.

```
============================ Coverage summary ============================
Statements   : 79.41% ( 54/68 )
Branches     : 76.31% ( 29/38 )
Functions    : 83.33% ( 25/30 )
Lines        : 78.46% ( 51/65 )
==========================================================================
```

You can also open `coverage/ng-demo/index.html` in your browser. You might notice that the `EditComponent` could use some additional coverage.

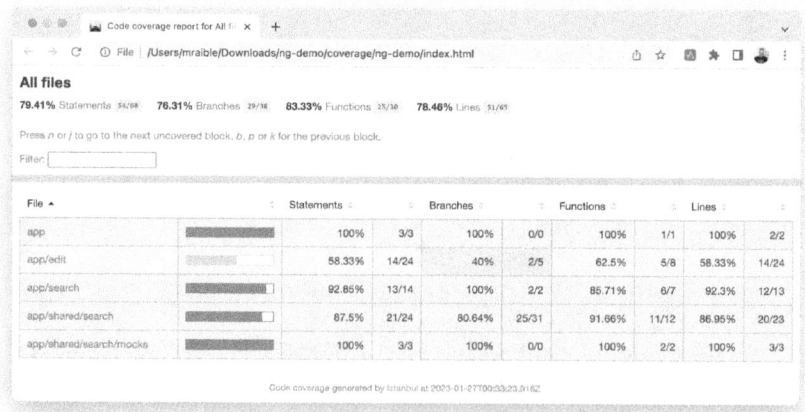

Figure 9. Test coverage

Continuous Integration

At the time of this writing, Angular CLI had no continuous integration support. This section shows you how to set up continuous integration with GitHub Actions and Jenkins.

 In the commands below, I use main as the branch name. If you're using master, I recommend you change your default branch name to main [https://www.hanselman.com/blog/easily-rename-your-git-default-branch-from-master-to-main].

```
git config --global init.defaultBranch main
```

GitHub Actions

If you've checked your project into GitHub, you can use GitHub Actions.

Create a .github/workflows/main.yml file. Add the following YAML to it. This will run both unit tests and integration tests with Cypress.

```
name: Demo CI

on: [push, pull_request]

jobs:
  build:
    name: Build and Test
    runs-on: ubuntu-latest
    steps:
      - name: Checkout
        uses: actions/checkout@v3
      - name: Use Node 18
        uses: actions/setup-node@v3
        with:
          node-version: 18
      - name: Install latest Chrome
        run: |
          sudo apt update
          sudo apt --only-upgrade install google-chrome-stable
          google-chrome --version
      - name: Install dependencies
        run: npm ci
      - name: Run unit tests
        run: xvfb-run npm test -- --watch=false
      - name: Run integration tests
        uses: cypress-io/github-action@v5
        with:
```

```
browser: chrome
start: npm start
install: false
wait-on: http://[::1]:4200
```

 See issue #634 [https://github.com/cypress-io/github-action/issues/634] for more information on the strange syntax for wait-on.

Check it in on a branch, create a pull request for that branch, and you should see your tests running.

Jenkins

If you've checked your project into source control, you can use Jenkins to automate testing.

1. Create a Jenkinsfile in the root directory and commit/push it.

```
node {
    def nodeHome = tool name: 'node-18', type:
'jenkins.plugins.nodejs.tools.NodeJSInstallation'
    env.PATH = "${nodeHome}/bin:${env.PATH}"

    stage('check tools') {
        sh "node -v"
        sh "npm -v"
    }

    stage('checkout') {
        checkout scm
    }

    stage('npm install') {
        sh "npm install"
    }

    stage('unit tests') {
        sh "npm test -- --watch=false"
    }

    stage('cypress tests') {
        sh "npm start &"
        sh "npm run cypress:run"
    }
}
```

2. Install Jenkins [https://www.jenkins.io/download/] on your hard drive and

start it:

```
java -jar jenkins.war
```

3. Log in to Jenkins at http://localhost:8080 and install the Node.js plugin.

4. Go to **Manage Jenkins** > **Global Tool Configuration** > **NodeJS**. Install and configure the name of your Node.js installation to match your build script.

5. Create a new project with **Dashboard** > **New Item** > **Pipeline** > **Pipeline script from SCM** (near the bottom). Point it at your project's repository and specify the main branch.

6. Click **Save**, then **Build Now** on the following screen.

Deployment to Heroku

This section shows how to deploy an Angular app to Heroku.

Create a Heroku account [https://signup.heroku.com/], install the heroku CLI [https://devcenter.heroku.com/articles/heroku-cli], and run heroku login.

Run heroku create to create an app on Heroku.

Create a config/nginx.conf.erb file with the configuration for secure headers and redirect all HTTP requests to HTTPS.

```
daemon off;
# Heroku dynos have at least 4 cores.
worker_processes <%= ENV['NGINX_WORKERS'] || 4 %>;

events {
    use epoll;
    accept_mutex on;
    worker_connections <%= ENV['NGINX_WORKER_CONNECTIONS'] || 1024 %>;
}

http {
    gzip on;
    gzip_comp_level 2;
    gzip_min_length 512;
    gzip_proxied any; # Heroku router sends Via header

    server_tokens off;

    log_format l2met 'measure#nginx.service=$request_time
```

```
request_id=$http_x_request_id';
    access_log <%= ENV['NGINX_ACCESS_LOG_PATH'] || 'logs/nginx/access.log' %>
l2met;
    error_log <%= ENV['NGINX_ERROR_LOG_PATH'] || 'logs/nginx/error.log' %>;

    include mime.types;
    default_type application/octet-stream;
    sendfile on;

    # Must read the body in 5 seconds.
    client_body_timeout <%= ENV['NGINX_CLIENT_BODY_TIMEOUT'] || 5 %>;

    server {
        listen <%= ENV["PORT"] %>;
        server_name _;
        keepalive_timeout 5;
        client_max_body_size <%= ENV['NGINX_CLIENT_MAX_BODY_SIZE'] || 1 %>M;

        root dist/ng-demo;
        index index.html;

        location / {
            try_files $uri /index.html;
        }

        add_header Content-Security-Policy "default-src 'self'; script-src
'self' 'unsafe-eval'; style-src 'self' 'unsafe-inline'; img-src 'self' data:;
font-src 'self' data:; frame-ancestors 'none'; connect-src 'self'
https://*.auth0.com https://*.herokuapp.com";
        add_header Referrer-Policy "no-referrer, strict-origin-when-cross-
origin";
        add_header Strict-Transport-Security "max-age=63072000;
includeSubDomains";
        add_header X-Content-Type-Options nosniff;
        add_header X-Frame-Options DENY;
        add_header X-XSS-Protection "1; mode=block";
        add_header Permissions-Policy "geolocation=(self), microphone=(),
accelerometer=(), camera=()";
    }
}
```

 In this code, you might notice that some https URLs are allowed in the content security policy. Those are there so this app can make XHR requests to those domains when that functionality is added.

For config/nginx.conf.erb to be read, you have to use the Heroku NGINX buildpack [https://elements.heroku.com/buildpacks/heroku/heroku-buildpack-nginx].

Add a Procfile to the root of your project.

```
web: bin/start-nginx-solo
```

Commit your changes to Git, add the Node.js + NGINX buildpack, and redeploy your Angular app using git push.

```
git add .
git commit -m "Configure secure headers and nginx buildpack"
heroku buildpacks:add heroku/nodejs
heroku buildpacks:add heroku-community/nginx
git push heroku main
```

View the application in your browser with heroku open. Try your app's URL on https://securityheaders.com to be pleasantly surprised.

💡 You can watch your app's logs using heroku logs --tail.

Styling with Bootstrap

To integrate Bootstrap and Bootstrap widgets into your Angular CLI-generated app, install NG Bootstrap [https://ng-bootstrap.github.io/].

```
ng add @ng-bootstrap/ng-bootstrap
```

This will install Bootstrap, NG Bootstrap, @angular/localize, and @popperjs/core. It will also configure Angular to use Bootstrap for CSS and import NgbModule in app.module.ts.

Then, change your HTML templates to use Bootstrap classes. For example, change app.component.html to be the following:

Listing 42. src/app/app.component.html

```
<nav class="navbar navbar-light bg-secondary">
  <div class="container-fluid">
    <a class="navbar-brand text-light" href="#">Welcome to {{ title }}!</a>
  </div>
</nav>
<div class="container-fluid">
  <router-outlet></router-outlet>
</div>
```

You'll also need to change its test to look for nav instead of h1.

Listing 43. src/app/app.component.spec.ts

```
expect(compiled.querySelector('nav')?.textContent)
  .toContain('Welcome to ng-demo!');
```

Update `search.component.html` to add a top margin to the H2, put the form in a grid layout, and add classes to input/button/table elements.

Listing 44. src/app/search/search.component.html

```html
<h2 class="mt-2">Search</h2>
<form class="row g-2">
  <div class="col-auto">
    <input type="search" name="query" [(ngModel)]="query"
(keyup.enter)="search()"
           placeholder="Search" class="form-control ml-2 mr-2">
  </div>
  <div class="col-auto">
    <button type="button" (click)="search()" class="btn btn-
primary">Search</button>
  </div>
</form>
<table *ngIf="searchResults?.length" class="table">
  <thead>
  <tr>
    <th>Name</th>
    <th>Phone</th>
    <th>Address</th>
  </tr>
  </thead>
  <tbody>
  <tr *ngFor="let person of searchResults; let i=index">
    <td><a [routerLink]="['/edit', person.id]">{{person.name}}</a></td>
    <td>{{person.phone}}</td>
    <td>{{person.address.street}}<br/>
      {{person.address.city}}, {{person.address.state}}
{{person.address.zip}}
    </td>
  </tr>
  </tbody>
</table>
```

Make similar changes to `edit.component.html`:

Listing 45. src/app/edit/edit.component.html

```html
<div *ngIf="person" class="col-8">
  <h3 class="mt-2">{{person.name}}</h3>
  <form (ngSubmit)="save()" #editForm="ngForm">
    <div>
```

```
      <label>Id:</label>
      {{person.id}}
    </div>
    <div class="form-group">
      <label for="name">Name:</label>
      <input [(ngModel)]="person.name" name="name" id="name"
placeholder="Name" required class="form-control" #name="ngModel"
        [ngClass]="{'is-invalid': name.touched && name.invalid, 'is-
valid': name.touched && name.valid}"/>
      <div [hidden]="name.valid || name.pristine" style="display: block"
class="invalid-feedback">
        Name is required
      </div>
    </div>
    <div class="form-group">
      <label>Phone:</label>
      <input [(ngModel)]="person.phone" name="phone" id="phone"
placeholder="Phone" class="form-control"/>
    </div>
    <fieldset class="form-group">
      <legend class="col-form-legend">Address:</legend>
      <address>
        <input [(ngModel)]="person.address.street" name="street" id="street"
class="form-control mb-2">
        <div class="row">
          <div class="col-6">
            <input [(ngModel)]="person.address.city" name="city" id="city"
class="form-control">
          </div>
          <div class="col-3">
            <input [(ngModel)]="person.address.state" name="state" id="state"
size="2" class="form-control">
          </div>
          <div class="col-3">
            <input [(ngModel)]="person.address.zip" name="zip" id="zip"
size="5" class="form-control">
          </div>
        </div>
      </address>
    </fieldset>
    <button type="submit" id="save" class="btn btn-primary"
[disabled]="!editForm.form.valid">Save</button>
    <button (click)="cancel()" id="cancel" class="btn btn-
light">Cancel</button>
  </form>
</div>
```

After modifying your templates, the edit screen will look as follows:

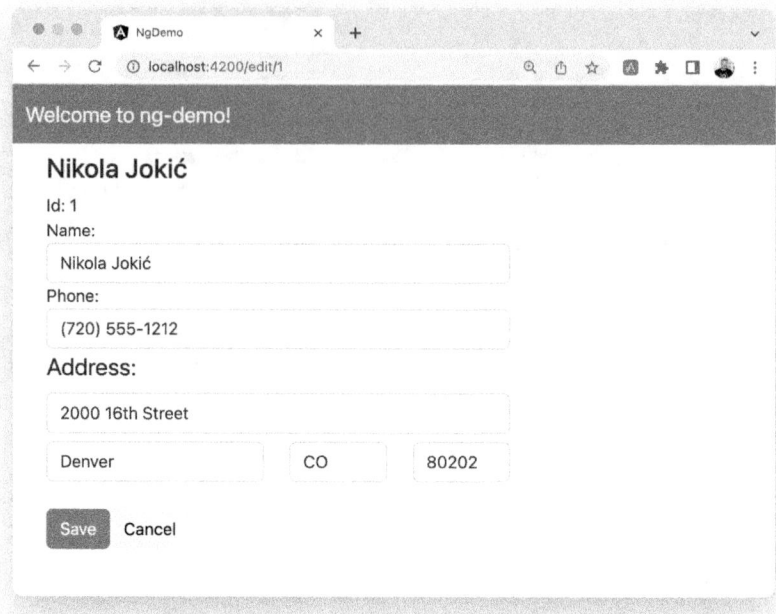

Figure 10. Bootstrap

Styling with Angular Material

To integrate Angular Material into your Angular CLI-generated app, install Angular Material [https://material.angular.io/].

```
ng add @angular/material
```

When prompted for the theme, pick the one you prefer, using the links to preview them. Accept the defaults for the other questions.

Add the relevant Material modules as imports in app.module.ts:

Listing 46. src/app/app.module.ts

```
import { MatButtonModule } from '@angular/material/button';
import { MatListModule } from '@angular/material/list';
import { MatInputModule } from '@angular/material/input';
import { MatIconModule } from '@angular/material/icon';
import { MatToolbarModule } from '@angular/material/toolbar';

@NgModule({
  ...
```

```
  imports: [
    ...
    MatButtonModule,
    MatIconModule,
    MatInputModule,
    MatListModule,
    MatToolbarModule
  ],
  ...
})
```

Then, change your HTML templates to use Material components. For example, change <h1> in app.component.html to <mat-toolbar>.

Listing 47. src/app/app.component.html

```
<mat-toolbar>Welcome to {{ title }}!</mat-toolbar>
```

You'll also need to change this component's test to import Material modules and look for mat-toolbar instead of h1.

Listing 48. src/app/app.component.spec.ts

```
import { TestBed } from '@angular/core/testing';
import { MatListModule } from '@angular/material/list';
import { MatToolbarModule } from '@angular/material/toolbar';

describe('AppComponent', () => {
  beforeEach(async () => {
    await TestBed.configureTestingModule({
      imports: [
        RouterTestingModule,
        MatListModule,
        MatToolbarModule
      ],
      declarations: [
        AppComponent
      ],
    }).compileComponents();
  });

  ...
  it('should render title', () => {
    ...
    expect(compiled.querySelector('mat-toolbar')?.textContent)
      .toContain('Welcome to ng-demo!');
  });
}
```

Update `search.component.html` to use Material components.

Listing 49. src/app/search/search.component.html

```html
<h2>Search</h2>
<form>
  <mat-form-field>
    <input matInput type="search" name="query" placeholder="Search"
           [(ngModel)]="query" (keyup.enter)="search()">
  </mat-form-field>
  <button mat-mini-fab (click)="search()"><mat-icon>search</mat-
icon></button>
</form>
<mat-list *ngIf="searchResults?.length" flex>
  <mat-list-item *ngFor="let person of searchResults; let i=index">
    <div class="mat-list-item-text">
      <div mat-line><a [routerLink]="['/edit',
person.id]">{{person.name}}</a></div>
      <div mat-line>{{person.phone}}</div>
      <div mat-line>{{person.address.street}}<br/>
        {{person.address.city}}, {{person.address.state}}
{{person.address.zip}}</div>
    </div>
  </mat-list-item>
</mat-list>
```

Update this component's test to be aware of these components.

Listing 50. src/app/search/search.component.spec.ts

```typescript
import { NoopAnimationsModule } from '@angular/platform-browser/animations';
import { MatListModule } from '@angular/material/list';
import { MatIconModule } from '@angular/material/icon';
import { MatInputModule } from '@angular/material/input';

describe('SearchComponent', () => {
  ...
  beforeEach(async () => {
    ...

    await TestBed.configureTestingModule({
      ...
      imports: [FormsModule, RouterTestingModule, HttpClientTestingModule,
        MatListModule, MatIconModule, MatInputModule, NoopAnimationsModule]
    }).compileComponents();
  });

  ...
}
```

Replace the plain ol' HTML inputs in edit.component.html with Material components.

Listing 51. src/app/edit/edit.component.html

```
<div *ngIf="person">
  <h3>{{person.name}}</h3>
  <form (ngSubmit)="save()" #editForm="ngForm">
    <div>
      <label>Id:</label>
      {{person.id}}
    </div>
    <p>
      <mat-form-field>
        <input matInput [(ngModel)]="person.name" name="name" id="name"
placeholder="Name" required/>
      </mat-form-field>
    </p>
    <p>
      <mat-form-field>
        <input matInput [(ngModel)]="person.phone" name="phone" id="phone"
placeholder="Phone"/>
      </mat-form-field>
    </p>
    <table>
      <tr>
        <td>
          <mat-form-field>
            <input matInput placeholder="Address"
[(ngModel)]="person.address.street" name="street" id="street">
          </mat-form-field>
        </td>
        <td>
          <mat-form-field>
            <input matInput placeholder="City"
[(ngModel)]="person.address.city" name="city" id="city">
          </mat-form-field>
        </td>
      </tr>
      <tr>
        <td>
          <mat-form-field>
            <input matInput placeholder="State" #state
[(ngModel)]="person.address.state" name="state" id="state" maxlength="2">
          </mat-form-field>
        </td>
        <td>
          <mat-form-field>
            <input matInput placeholder="Zip" #postalCode maxlength="5"
[(ngModel)]="person.address.zip" name="zip" id="zip">
            <mat-hint align="end">{{postalCode.value.length}} / 5</mat-hint>
          </mat-form-field>
```

```
        </td>
      </tr>
    </table>

    <button mat-raised-button type="submit" color="primary" id="save"
            [disabled]="!editForm.form.valid">Save</button>
    <button mat-button (click)="cancel(); false" id="cancel">Cancel</button>
  </form>
</div>
```

And import modules used in its test.

Listing 52. src/app/edit/edit.component.spec.ts

```
import { MatInputModule } from '@angular/material/input';
import { NoopAnimationsModule } from '@angular/platform-browser/animations';

describe('EditComponent', () => {
  ...
  beforeEach(async () => {
    ...

    await TestBed.configureTestingModule({
      ...
      imports: [FormsModule, HttpClientTestingModule, MatInputModule,
NoopAnimationsModule]
    }).compileComponents();
  });

  ...
}
```

After completing these changes, the edit screen will look as follows:

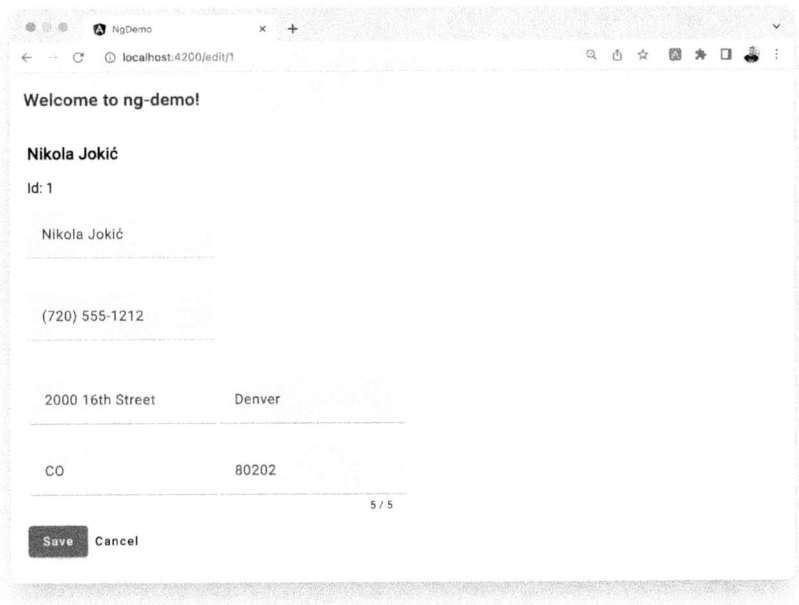

Figure 11. Angular Material

Run npm test to confirm your unit tests pass.

For Cypress tests, you must modify the list reference in search.spec.ts and edit.spec.ts to look for Material components instead of table rows.

```
const list = cy.get('app-search mat-list mat-list-item');
```

Add Auth with OpenID Connect

To add authentication with OpenID Connect, you'll first need a free Auth0 account [https://auth0.com/signup]. Install the Auth0 CLI [https://github.com/auth0/auth0-cli#installation] and run auth0 login to register your account. Then, run auth0 apps create. Specify a name and description of your choosing. Choose **Single Page Web Application** and use http://localhost:4200/home for the Callback URL. Specify http://localhost:4200 for the rest of the URLs.

Add OIDC Authentication with OktaDev Schematics

Use OktaDev Schematics [https://github.com/oktadev/schematics] to add OAuth 2.0 and OpenID Connect (OIDC) support.

```
ng add @oktadev/schematics --auth0
```

You'll be prompted for an issuer and client ID. You should have these from the OIDC app you just created.

This process will perform the following steps:

1. Install the Auth0 Angular SDK [https://github.com/auth0/auth0-angular].

2. Add `src/app/auth-routing.module.ts` with your OIDC configuration and initialization logic.

3. Configure an `AuthHttpInterceptor` that adds an `Authorization` header with an access token to outbound requests.

4. Create a `HomeComponent` and configure it with authentication logic.

5. Update unit tests for `AppComponent` and `HomeComponent` to mock Auth0.

In addition to these changes, remove the default route from `app-routing.ts` and add a route guard to the `/search` and `/edit` routes.

Listing 53. src/app/app-routing.ts

```
import { AuthGuard } from '@auth0/auth0-angular';

const routes: Routes = [
  { path: 'search', component: SearchComponent, canActivate: [AuthGuard] },
  { path: 'edit/:id', component: EditComponent, canActivate: [AuthGuard] }
];
```

This is necessary because the `HomeComponent` has a default route configured in `src/app/auth-routing.ts`. The `AuthGuard` makes authentication required.

```
const routes: Routes = [
  { path: '', redirectTo: '/home', pathMatch: 'full' },
  {
    path: 'home',
    component: HomeComponent
  }
];
```

You'll also need to update the `app.component.spec.ts` file's last test to look for the correct welcome message.

```
it('should render title', () => {
```

```
const fixture = TestBed.createComponent(AppComponent);
fixture.detectChanges();
const compiled = fixture.nativeElement as HTMLElement;
expect(compiled.querySelector('h1')?.textContent)
  .toContain('Welcome to ng-demo!');
});
```

After making these changes, you should be able to run `ng serve` and see a login button at `http://localhost:4200/home`.

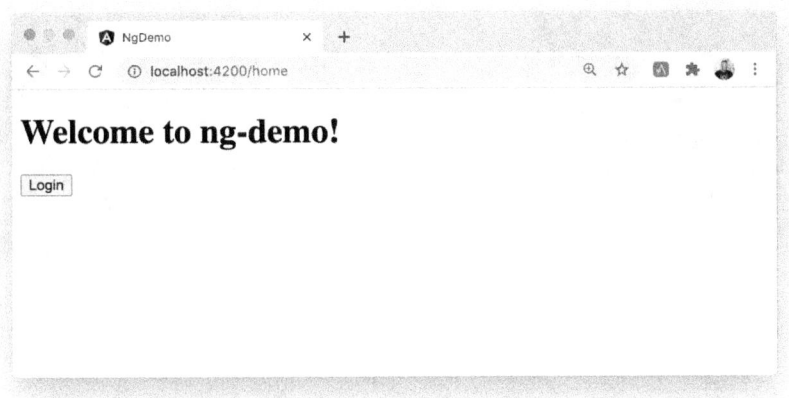

Figure 12. Auth0 login button

Click the **Login** button and sign in with one of the users that are configured in your Auth0 application or sign up as a new user.

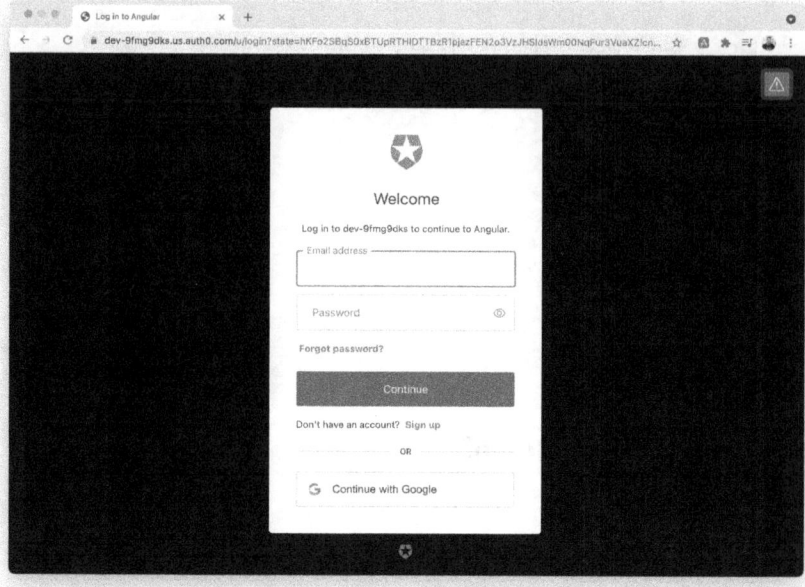

Figure 13. Auth0 login form

Display Authenticated User's Name

To display the authenticated user's name, you can use the user$ observable on the AuthService instance.

Modify home.component.html to display a welcome message to the user and provide them with a link to search.

Listing 54. src/app/home/home.component.html

```
<ng-container *ngIf="(auth.isAuthenticated$ | async) === false; else
signout">
  <button (click)="login()" id="login">Login</button>
</ng-container>
<ng-template #signout>
  <div *ngIf="auth.user$ | async as user">
    <h2>Welcome, {{user?.name}}!</h2>
    <p><a routerLink="/search" routerLinkActive="active">Search</a></p>
  </div>
  <button (click)="logout()" id="logout">Logout</button>
</ng-template>
```

Refresh your app, and you should see your name with a link to **Search**.

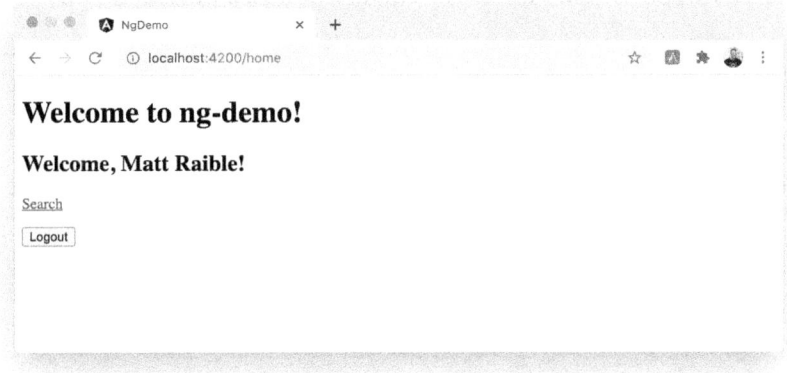

Figure 14. View after login

If you log out and manually navigate to `http://localhost:4200/search`, you'll be required to log in.

If everything works—congrats!

Add Authentication to Cypress tests

To make it so you can run your e2e tests with authentication, add a `signIn()` Cypress command in `cypress/support/commands.ts`.

```
Cypress.Commands.add('signIn', (username, password) => {
  Cypress.log({
    message: [`Authenticating: ${username}`],
    autoEnd: false,
  })

  cy.origin(Cypress.env('E2E_DOMAIN'), {args: {username, password}},
    ({username, password}) => {
      cy.get('input[name=username]').type(username);
      cy.get('input[name=password]').type(`${password}{enter}`, {log:
false});
    }
  )

  cy.url().should('equal', 'http://localhost:4200/home')
})
```

Then, in `cypress/support/e2e.ts`, uncomment the import for `commands` and specify `before()` and `after()` functions that log in and log out before each test.

```
import './commands';

beforeEach(() => {
  cy.visit('/')
  cy.get('#login').click()
  cy.signIn(
    Cypress.env('E2E_USERNAME'),
    Cypress.env('E2E_PASSWORD')
  )
})

afterEach(() => {
  cy.visit('/')
  cy.get('#logout').click()
})
```

Modify cypress/e2e/home.cy.ts to remove the line with cy.visit('/').

Next, configure your domain and credentials in cypress.config.ts.

```
"env": {
  "E2E_DOMAIN": "YOUR_AUTH0_DOMAIN",
  "E2E_USERNAME": "YOUR_AUTH0_USERNAME",
  "E2E_PASSWORD": "YOUR_AUTH0_PASSWORD"
},
```

Then, start your app (with ng serve) and run its Cypress tests in a separate terminal window.

```
npm run cypress:run
```

Don't Store Credentials in Source Control

In this example, I recommended you store your username and password in cypress.config.ts. This is convenient, but a bad practice.

You can solve it by using cypress.env.json [https://docs.cypress.io/guides/guides/environment-variables#Option-2-cypressenvjson].

Create a cypress.env.json file in your project's root folder with your Auth0 credentials in it.

```
{
  "E2E_DOMAIN": "<your domain>",
  "E2E_USERNAME": "<your username>",
```

```
  "E2E_PASSWORD": "<your password>"
}
```

Add *.env.json to your .gitignore file to prevent this file from being checked in.

Then, remove the env key from cypress.config.ts.

Now, npm run cypress:run should work as before.

Update GitHub Actions

If you're using GitHub Actions to test your project, you'll need to update the Cypress workflow to include your domain and credentials.

```
- name: Run integration tests
  uses: cypress-io/github-action@v5
  with:
    browser: chrome
    start: npm start
    install: false
    wait-on: http://[::1]:4200
  env:
    CYPRESS_E2E_DOMAIN: ${{ secrets.E2E_DOMAIN }}
    CYPRESS_E2E_USERNAME: ${{ secrets.E2E_USERNAME }}
    CYPRESS_E2E_PASSWORD: ${{ secrets.E2E_PASSWORD }}
```

Then, create repository secrets on GitHub for E2E_DOMAIN, E2E_USERNAME and E2E_PASSWORD.

It is also useful to upload screenshots of your test failures to GitHub. Add the following to your workflow.

```
- name: Upload screenshots on failure
  if: failure()
  uses: actions/upload-artifact@v3
  with:
    name: cypress-screenshots
    path: cypress/screenshots
```

You can then download the screenshots by going to a job's summary. From there, scroll down to the **Artifacts** section and click on the **cypress-screenshots** artifact.

Summary

I hope you've enjoyed this introduction to Angular. You learned how to create a basic application without worrying about the back end.

 You can download the code for this book's examples from InfoQ. The ng-demo directory has this chapter's completed example. There are also examples for Angular Material, Bootstrap, and Auth0.

In the next section, I'll show you how to use a modern back end to provide data, security, and production-ready features.

PART TWO

Integrate Angular with Spring Boot

In the first section, you learned about Angular and how to use it without having a back end. In this section, I'll show you how to use it with a Spring Boot back end.

Spring Boot is one of the most popular frameworks for developing Java applications and REST APIs. It also has first-class support for Kotlin!

What is Kotlin? It's an open source, statically typed, general-purpose programming language with type inference. Kotlin originated at JetBrains, the company behind IntelliJ IDEA, in 2010, and has been open source since 2012. Today, it is widely used to develop Android applications. At first glance, Kotlin looks like a more concise and streamlined version of Java.

When Kotlin was announced as an official Android development language at Google I/O in May 2017, it became the third language fully supported for Android, in addition to Java and C++. As of 2020, Kotlin is still most widely used on Android, with Google estimating that 70% of the top 1000 apps on the Play Store are written in Kotlin.

Spring Boot 1.0 was released on April 1, 2014, and revolutionized the way Java developers write Spring apps. Instead of writing a lot of boilerplate XML or JavaConfig with annotations, Spring Boot introduced the idea of pre-configured *starters* with smart defaults via auto-configuration.

Long story short, Angular, Kotlin, and Spring Boot are a match made in heaven!

Figure 15. Bootiful Angular

What's New in Angular?

Angular 15 is the version of Angular used in this book. It adds support for standalone components and optimized images using the `ngSrc` attribute. You can read more about its new features on the Angular Blog [https://blog.angular.io/angular-v15-is-now-available-df7be7f2f4c8].

If you have an existing app, you can update to the latest release of Angular using `ng update` command from the Angular CLI:

```
ng update @angular/cli @angular/core
```

What's New in Spring Boot?

Spring Boot 3.0 was released in November 2022. It requires Java 17, supports native images by default with GraalVM, improves observability with Micrometer, and adds support for Jakarta EE 10. You can read more about its new features on the Spring Blog [https://spring.io/blog/2022/11/24/spring-boot-3-0-goes-ga].

In this chapter, I'll show you how to build a note-taking application with Angular 15 and Spring Boot 3. Along the way, I'll do my best to weave in security tips and advice on how to make your apps more secure.

The Angular and Spring Boot projects release major versions every six months. Since Java does, too, this book might be a release or two behind when you're reading this. Both projects have great track records for backward compatibility, so there's a good chance everything will work on newer versions.

Please try newer versions at your own risk and email me if you find issues and/or solutions! I've been known to trade t-shirts for contributions.

Prerequisites:

- Node 18 [https://nodejs.org/]+

- Java 17 [https://adoptium.net/]+

- HTTPie [https://httpie.io/docs#installation]

To install Node and Java on a Mac, Linux, or Windows Subsystem for Linux (WSL), you can use Homebrew [https://docs.brew.sh/Installation].

```
brew install node
```

```
brew tap AdoptOpenJDK/openjdk
brew cask install adoptopenjdk17
```

You can also use SDKMAN! [https://sdkman.io] to install Java 17.

```
sdk install java
```

If you like to live on the bleeding edge, the latest version of the JDK should work too.

The previous section was an intro to Angular and showed you how it works without a back end. In this section, you'll create a new app that's more of a *real-world* application.

Create an Angular App

You should have installed the Angular CLI in the previous section. If you did not, do it now.

```
npm install -g @angular/cli@15
```

Then, create a directory on your hard drive called angular-spring-boot. Open a terminal window and navigate to this directory. Run the ng new command from Angular CLI to create a new Angular application.

```
ng new notes --routing --style css
```

In this command, --routing installs the Angular router, and --style css makes it use CSS (as opposed to Sass and Less) for stylesheets.

Depending on your internet speed and hardware, this process will take a minute or two. Once it's finished, navigate into the directory and run ng serve.

```
cd notes
ng serve
```

Open your browser to http://localhost:4200, and you'll see the default homepage.

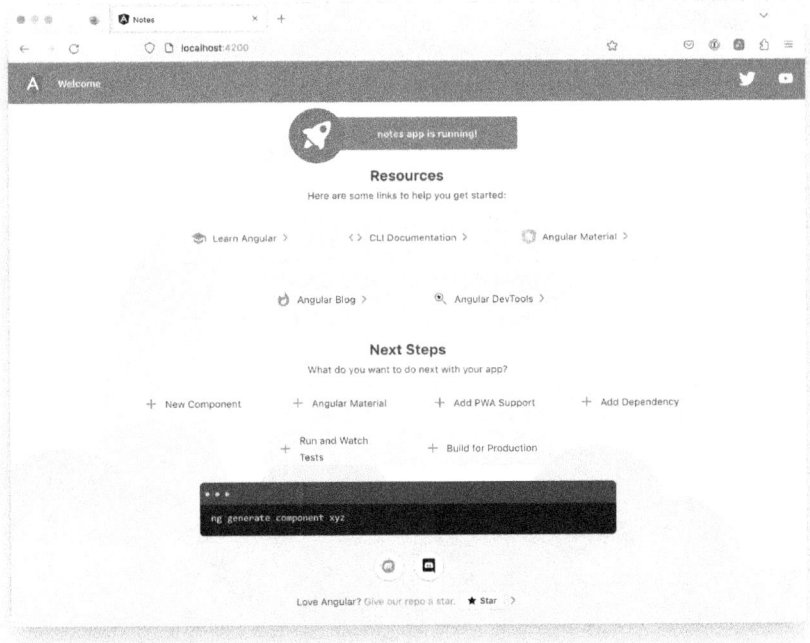

Figure 16. Angular default homepage

Stop the `ng serve` process using `Ctrl+C` in your terminal.

Add Authentication using OpenID Connect

OpenID Connect (also called OIDC) is an identity layer based on the OAuth 2.0 specification. It leverages JSON Web Tokens (JWT) to provide an ID token and other features like discoverability and a `/userinfo` endpoint. In the first section, I showed you how to use Auth0 as an identity provider. Let's continue that path because Auth0 is excellent and one of the easiest identity providers to use.

To add OIDC login support to your Angular app, you'll need a free Auth0 account [https://auth0.com/signup]. Install the Auth0 CLI [https://github.com/auth0/auth0-cli] and run `auth0 login` to authorize your device.

Then, create a new OIDC app with `auth0 apps create`. Specify the name, type, callback URLs, and logout redirect URL.

```
auth0 apps create \
  --name "Angular" \
  --description "Angular OIDC App" \
```

```
--type spa \
--callbacks http://localhost:4200/home \
--logout-urls http://localhost:4200 \
--origins http://localhost:4200 \
--web-origins http://localhost:4200
```

When you create Single Page Applications (SPAs) with the Auth0 CLI, authorization code flow with PKCE (Proof Key for Code Exchange) is selected by default. This setting provides the maximum level of security you can currently have for single-page apps when using OIDC for auth.

 To learn more about PKCE (pronounced "pixy"), see Implement the OAuth 2.0 Authorization Code with PKCE Flow [https://developer.okta.com/blog/2019/08/22/okta-authjs-pkce].

Copy your client ID and issuer URI (from the Auth0 CLI's output) into the following command.

```
ng add @oktadev/schematics --auth0 --issuer=$issuer --clientId=$clientId
```

This command adds Auth0's Angular SDK and configures OIDC authentication for your app.

Figure 17. OktaDev Schematics in Action

The process creates a `home.component.ts` that has authentication logic, as well as a template that renders login and logout buttons.

Listing 55. src/app/home/home.component.ts

```
import { Component, Inject } from '@angular/core';
import { AuthService } from '@auth0/auth0-angular';
import { DOCUMENT } from '@angular/common';

@Component({
  selector: 'app-home',
  templateUrl: './home.component.html',
  styleUrls: ['./home.component.css']
})
export class HomeComponent {

  constructor(public auth: AuthService, @Inject(DOCUMENT) private doc:
Document) {
  }

  login(): void {
    this.auth.loginWithRedirect();
  }

  logout(): void {
    this.auth.logout({
      logoutParams: {
        returnTo: this.doc.location.origin
      }
    });
  }
}
```

Listing 56. src/app/home/home.component.html

```
<div>
  <button *ngIf="(auth.isAuthenticated$ | async) === false"
    (click)="login()">Login</button>
  <button *ngIf="auth.isAuthenticated$ | async"
    (click)="logout()">Logout</button>
</div>
```

The auth-routing.module.ts configures an HttpInterceptor and its
allowedList to add an access token to outgoing HTTP requests.

Listing 57. src/app/auth-routing.module.ts

```
const config = {
  domain: '...',
  clientId: '...',
  authorizationParams: {
    redirect_uri: window.location.origin + '/home',
  },
```

```
  httpInterceptor: {
    allowedList: ['/api/*']
  },
};
```

You'll need to update this configuration to add an `audience` parameter and so it'll add an access token when sending requests to your Spring Boot API.

Listing 58. src/app/auth-routing.module.ts

```
const config = {
  authorizationParams: {
    audience: 'https://<your-auth0-domain>/api/v2/',
  },
  httpInterceptor: {
    allowedList: ['http://localhost:8080/*']
  },
};
```

Start your app again using the `ng serve` command, open a private/incognito window to `http://localhost:4200`, and you'll see a **Login** button in the bottom left.

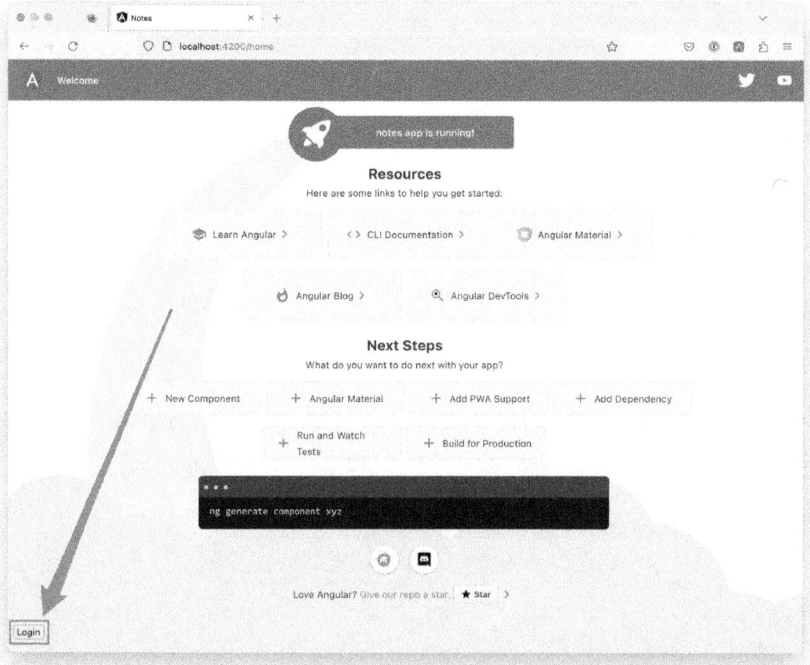

Figure 18. Login button

Click on it, and you'll be redirected to Auth0 to log in.

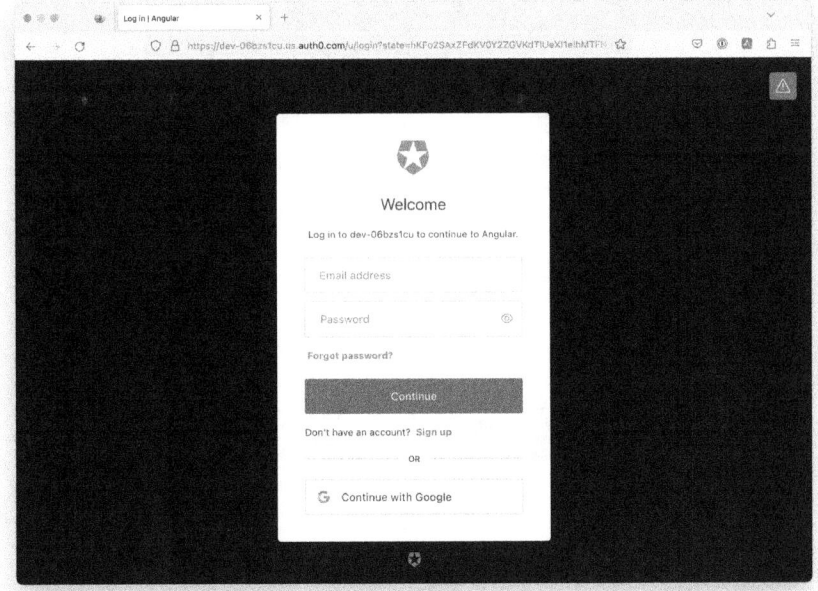

Figure 19. Auth0 Login form

Enter valid credentials, and you'll be redirected back to your app. There will now be a **Logout** button, indicating that you've authenticated successfully.

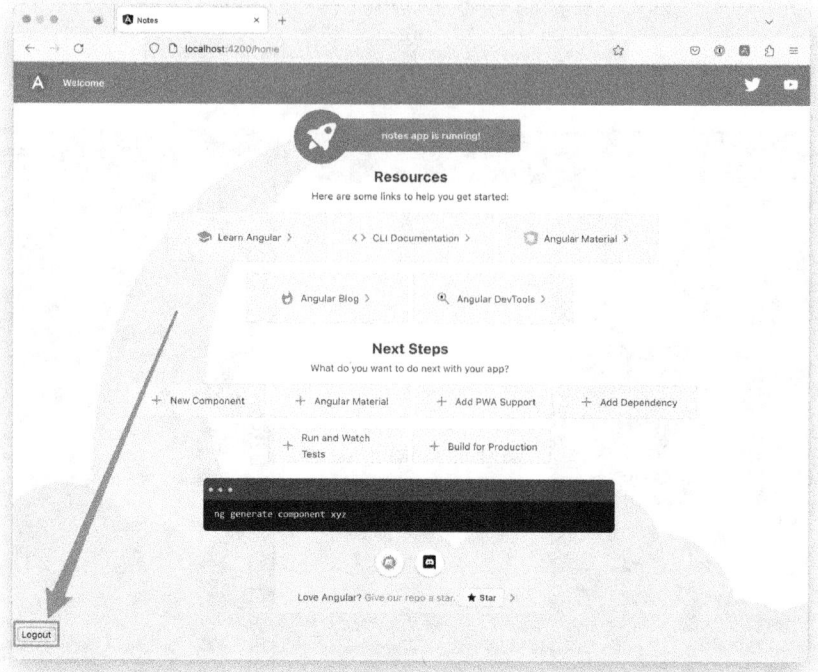

Figure 20. Logout button

Now that you've created a secure Angular app let's create a Spring Boot app to serve up data with a REST API.

Create a Spring Boot App

The good folks at VMWare created start.spring.io [https://start.spring.io] to help you create Spring Boot apps quickly with minimal fuss. This site is a Spring Boot app with a REST API you can use with HTTPie.

Kotlin is an intriguing language for Spring developers because it reduces boilerplate code and allows succinct, effective code. Kotlin is 100% interoperable with Java, so you can continue to use the Java libraries and frameworks you know and love. Not only that, but Spring has first-class support for Kotlin.

Create a new Spring Boot app that uses Kotlin and Gradle, and has the necessary dependencies to create a secure CRUD API.

```
https start.spring.io/starter.zip type==gradle-project-kotlin \
  language==kotlin bootVersion==3.0.4 \
  artifactId==notes-api groupId==com.okta.developer \
  packageName==com.okta.developer.notes \
  dependencies==h2,data-jpa,data-rest,okta,validation,web -d
```

 You can remove the bootVersion parameter to use the latest version of Spring Boot. Or, you can change it to a newer version, and it *should* work. The value used here has been QA'd and is guaranteed to work.

Run this command in a terminal, and a `notes-api.zip` file will be downloaded. Expand it into the `angular-spring-boot/notes-api` directory.

```
unzip notes-api.zip -d angular-spring-boot/notes-api
```

Secure Spring Boot with Spring Security

Because you selected Okta as a dependency, you'll need to create an OIDC app for it to authenticate with OpenID Connect. You could use the client ID from your Angular app, but if you ever want to allow people to log in to your Spring Boot app, it'll need its own OIDC app.

The OIDC integration you added to your Angular app allows you to authenticate a user and receive an access token. You can use this access token to securely communicate with a back end that is configured to use the same issuer. This is done by using an HTTP interceptor that adds it in an `Authorization` header as a bearer token.

Open a terminal and navigate to your Spring Boot app's directory. Create an OIDC app for Spring Boot with the following command:

```
auth0 apps create \
  --name "Spring Boot" \
  --description "Spring Boot OIDC App" \
  --type regular \
  --callbacks http://localhost:8080/login/oauth2/code/okta \
  --logout-urls http://localhost:8080 \
  --reveal-secrets
```

Copy the results of the previous command into an `.okta.env` file. You'll need to replace the placeholders with your values.

```
export OKTA_OAUTH2_ISSUER=https://<your-auth0-domain>/
export OKTA_OAUTH2_CLIENT_ID=<your-client-id>
export OKTA_OAUTH2_CLIENT_SECRET=<your-client-secret>
export OKTA_OAUTH2_AUDIENCE=https://<your-auth0-domain>/api/v2/
```

After replacing the <···> placeholders with your values, run source .okta.env to set these environment variables.

Then start your app using ./gradlew bootRun. Open http://localhost:8080 in a browser, and you'll be redirected to Auth0 to sign in.

If you don't get prompted, it's because you're already logged in. Try it in an incognito window to see the full login flow.

Spring Boot as an OAuth 2.0 Resource Server

Your Spring Boot API is now secure, and it's configured to look for an Authorization header with an access token in it. The Okta Spring Boot starter configures your Spring Boot API as an OAuth 2.0 resource server by default and enables login.

To override the default configuration, create a SecurityConfiguration.kt class in the same directory as DemoApplication.kt:

Listing 59. notes-api/src/main/kotlin/com/okta/developer/notes/SecurityConfiguration.kt

```
package com.okta.developer.notes

import org.springframework.context.annotation.Bean
import org.springframework.context.annotation.Configuration
import org.springframework.security.config.Customizer.withDefaults
import
org.springframework.security.config.annotation.web.builders.HttpSecurity
import org.springframework.security.web.SecurityFilterChain

@Configuration
class SecurityConfiguration {

    @Bean
    fun webSecurity(http: HttpSecurity): SecurityFilterChain {
        http
            .authorizeHttpRequests { authz ->
                authz.anyRequest().authenticated()
            }
            .oauth2Login(withDefaults())
```

```
            .oauth2ResourceServer().jwt()

        return http.build()
    }
}
```

 The oauth2Login() configuration is not necessary for this example to work. It's only needed if you want to require authentication from a browser and can be useful to test logging in without a client.

Spring Data REST

Start by creating a new Note entity in DemoApplication.kt.

*Listing 60. notes-
api/src/main/kotlin/com/okta/developer/notes/DemoApplication.kt*

```
package com.okta.developer.notes

import com.fasterxml.jackson.annotation.JsonIgnore
import org.springframework.boot.autoconfigure.SpringBootApplication
import org.springframework.boot.runApplication
import jakarta.persistence.Entity
import jakarta.persistence.GeneratedValue
import jakarta.persistence.Id

@SpringBootApplication
class DemoApplication

fun main(args: Array<String>) {
    runApplication<DemoApplication>(*args)
}

@Entity
data class Note(@Id @GeneratedValue var id: Long? = null,
                var title: String? = null,
                var text: String? = null,
                @JsonIgnore var username: String? = null)
```

Kotlin's data classes [https://kotlinlang.org/docs/reference/data-classes.html] are built to hold data. By adding the data keyword, your class will get equals(), hashCode(), toString(), and a copy() function. The Type? = null syntax means the arguments are nullable when creating a new instance of the class.

Create a NotesRepository for persisting the data in your notes. Add the following lines of code just below your Note entity.

```
@RepositoryRestResource
interface NotesRepository : JpaRepository<Note, Long>
```

The extends syntax differs from Java and is a lot more concise (a colon instead of extends). If your IDE doesn't automatically add imports, you must add the following at the top of the file.

```
import org.springframework.data.jpa.repository.JpaRepository
import org.springframework.data.rest.core.annotation.RepositoryRestResource
```

To automatically add the username to a note when it's created, add a RepositoryEventHandler that is invoked before creating the record.

```
@Component
@RepositoryEventHandler(Note::class)
class AddUserToNote {

    @HandleBeforeCreate
    fun handleCreate(note: Note) {
        val username: String =
SecurityContextHolder.getContext().authentication.name
        note.username = username
        println("Creating note: $note")
    }
}
```

The imports for this class are:

```
import org.springframework.data.rest.core.annotation.HandleBeforeCreate
import org.springframework.data.rest.core.annotation.RepositoryEventHandler
import org.springframework.security.core.context.SecurityContextHolder
import org.springframework.stereotype.Component
```

Create a DataInitializer.kt class that populates the database with some default data on startup.

Listing 61. notes-api/src/main/kotlin/com/okta/developer/notes/DataInitializer.kt

```
package com.okta.developer.notes

import org.springframework.boot.ApplicationArguments
```

```
import org.springframework.boot.ApplicationRunner
import org.springframework.stereotype.Component

@Component
class DataInitializer(val repository: NotesRepository) : ApplicationRunner {

    @Throws(Exception::class)
    override fun run(args: ApplicationArguments) {
        listOf("Note 1", "Note 2", "Note 3").forEach {
            repository.save(Note(title = it, username = "user"))
        }
        repository.findAll().forEach { println(it) }
    }
}
```

Restart your Spring Boot app, and you should see the following printed to your console on startup.

```
Note(id=1, title=Note 1, text=null, username=user)
Note(id=2, title=Note 2, text=null, username=user)
Note(id=3, title=Note 3, text=null, username=user)
```

Create a UserController.kt class (in the same directory as DemoApplication.kt) and use it to filter notes by the currently logged-in user. While you're at it, add a /user endpoint that returns the user's information.

Listing 62. notes-api/src/main/kotlin/com/okta/developer/notes/UserController.kt

```
package com.okta.developer.notes

import org.springframework.security.core.annotation.AuthenticationPrincipal
import org.springframework.security.oauth2.core.oidc.user.OidcUser
import org.springframework.web.bind.annotation.GetMapping
import org.springframework.web.bind.annotation.RestController
import java.security.Principal

@RestController
class UserController(val repository: NotesRepository) {

    @GetMapping("/user/notes")
    fun notes(principal: Principal): List<Note> {
        println("Fetching notes for user: ${principal.name}")
        return repository.findAllByUsername(principal.name)
    }

    @GetMapping("/user")
```

```
    fun user(@AuthenticationPrincipal user: OidcUser): OidcUser {
        return user
    }
}
```

The `findAllByUser()` method doesn't exist on `NotesRepository`, so you'll need to add it. Thanks to Spring Data JPA, all you need to do is add the method definition to the interface, and it will handle generating the finder method in the implementation.

```
interface NotesRepository : JpaRepository<Note, Long> {
    fun findAllByUsername(name: String): List<Note>
}
```

To prevent conflicting paths with the REST endpoints created by `@RepositoryRestResource`, set the base path to `/api` in `application.properties`.

```
spring.data.rest.base-path=/api
```

Restart your Spring Boot app, navigate to `http://localhost:8080/user`, and you'll see a whole plethora of details about your account. Opening `http://localhost:8080/api/notes` will show the default notes entered by the `DataInitializer` component.

CORS Integration

For your Angular app (on port 4200) to communicate with your Spring Boot app (on port 8080), you have to enable CORS (cross-origin resource sharing). You can do this by updating your `SecurityConfiguration` to have `http.cors()` and defining a `corsConfigurationSource` bean.

```
package com.okta.developer.notes

...
import org.springframework.web.cors.CorsConfiguration
import org.springframework.web.cors.CorsConfigurationSource
import org.springframework.web.cors.UrlBasedCorsConfigurationSource

@Configuration
class SecurityConfiguration {

    @Bean
    fun webSecurity(http: HttpSecurity): SecurityFilterChain {
```

```
        ...
        http.cors()
        return http.build()
    }

    @Bean
    fun corsConfigurationSource(): CorsConfigurationSource {
        val source = UrlBasedCorsConfigurationSource()
        val config = CorsConfiguration()
        config.allowCredentials = true
        config.allowedOrigins = listOf("http://localhost:4200")
        config.allowedMethods = listOf("*")
        config.allowedHeaders = listOf("*")
        source.registerCorsConfiguration("/**", config)
        return source
    }
}
```

Restart your Spring Boot app after adding this bean.

Now that your API is working, it's time to develop a UI with Angular!

CRUD in Angular

Angular Schematics is a workflow tool that allows you to manipulate any project that has a package.json. Angular CLI is based on Schematics. OktaDev Schematics uses Schematics to update and add new files to projects. There's even an Angular CRUD [https://github.com/manfredsteyer/angular-crud] schematic!

Angular CRUD allows you to generate CRUD (create, read, update, and delete) screens and associated files from JSON.

In your Angular notes app, install angular-crud using npm:

```
npm i -D angular-crud@3
```

Then create a src/app/note directory.

```
mkdir -p src/app/note
```

Then, in that directory, create a model.json file that defines metadata used when generating files.

Listing 63. src/app/note/model.json

```json
{
  "title": "Notes",
  "entity": "note",
  "api": {
    "url": "http://localhost:8080/api/notes"
  },
  "filter": [
    "title"
  ],
  "fields": [
    {
      "name": "id",
      "label": "Id",
      "isId": true,
      "readonly": true,
      "type": "number"
    },
    {
      "name": "title",
      "type": "string",
      "label": "Title"
    },
    {
      "name": "text",
      "type": "string",
      "label": "Text"
    }
  ]
}
```

Then, run the command below to generate CRUD screens.

```
ng g angular-crud:crud-module note --style bootstrap
```

You will see the following output:

```
CREATE src/app/note/note-filter.ts (42 bytes)
CREATE src/app/note/note.module.ts (659 bytes)
CREATE src/app/note/note.routes.ts (346 bytes)
CREATE src/app/note/note.service.spec.ts (607 bytes)
CREATE src/app/note/note.service.ts (1774 bytes)
CREATE src/app/note/note.ts (72 bytes)
CREATE src/app/note/note-edit/note-edit.component.html (1007 bytes)
CREATE src/app/note/note-edit/note-edit.component.spec.ts (978 bytes)
CREATE src/app/note/note-edit/note-edit.component.ts (1527 bytes)
CREATE src/app/note/note-list/note-list.component.html (1601 bytes)
CREATE src/app/note/note-list/note-list.component.spec.ts (978 bytes)
```

```
CREATE src/app/note/note-list/note-list.component.ts (1116 bytes)
UPDATE src/app/app.module.ts (540 bytes)
```

This schematic creates a `NotesModule`, routes a service to communicate with the API, and list/edit screens for viewing and editing notes. Open the generated `note.routes.ts` file, and protect the routes it creates with `AuthGuard`.

Listing 64. src/app/note/note.routes.ts

```
import { Routes } from '@angular/router';
import { NoteListComponent } from './note-list/note-list.component';
import { NoteEditComponent } from './note-edit/note-edit.component';
import { AuthGuard } from '@auth0/auth0-angular';

export const NOTE_ROUTES: Routes = [
  {
    path: 'notes',
    component: NoteListComponent,
    canActivate: [AuthGuard],
  },
  {
    path: 'notes/:id',
    component: NoteEditComponent,
    canActivate: [AuthGuard]
  }
];
```

Add a link to the `NoteListComponent` in `src/app/home/home.component.html`.

```
<div>
  <button *ngIf="(auth.isAuthenticated$ | async) === false"
(click)="login()">Login</button>
  <p><a routerLink="/notes" *ngIf="auth.isAuthenticated$ | async">View
Notes</a></p>
  <button *ngIf="auth.isAuthenticated$ | async"
(click)="logout()">Logout</button>
</div>
```

Change `src/app/app.component.html` to be as simple as it can be.

```
<h1>{{ title }} app is running!</h1>

<router-outlet></router-outlet>
```

 If you want `npm` test to pass after modifying this

template, you'll need to change `app.component.spec.ts` to look for `querySelector('h1')` instead of `querySelector('.content span')`.

Run `ng serve` (and make sure your Spring Boot app is running, too).

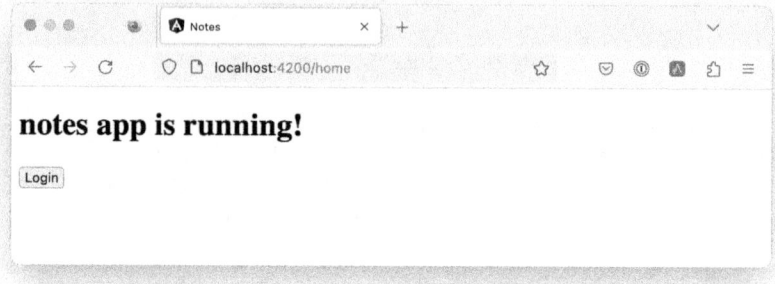

Figure 21. Notes App Login

Log in, and you should see a **View Notes** link.

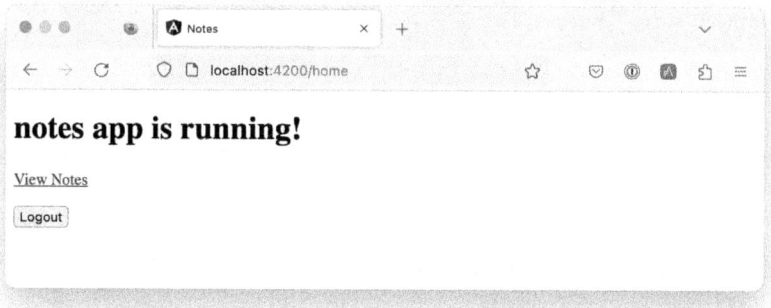

Figure 22. Notes Link

Click on the link, and you'll see a list screen like the one below. No notes are displayed because you haven't created any notes tied to your user.

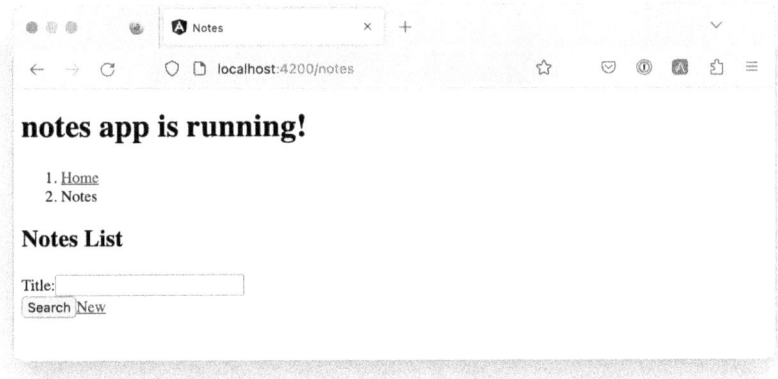

Figure 23. Notes List

Click on the **New** link to add a new note.

Figure 24. Notes Detail

Add a new note, and you'll see a message like this in your back-end console.

```
Creating note: Note(id=null, title=1st note, text=Wahoo!,
username=auth0|61bcbc76f64d4a0072af8a1d)
```

You still won't see notes in the list. You need to change the `NoteService` to call the `/user/notes` endpoint to get your notes.

Listing 65. notes/src/app/note/note.service.ts

```
find(filter: NoteFilter): Observable<Note[]> {
  const params = {
    'title': filter.title,
  }; const userNotes = 'http://localhost:8080/user/notes';
  return this.http.get<Note[]>(userNotes, {params, headers});
}
```

Now you'll see your notes listed. Nice work!

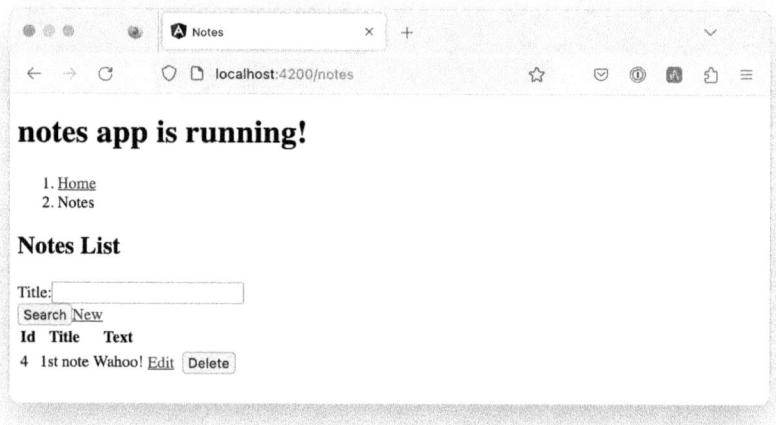

Figure 25. Notes User List

You might be wondering how the `NoteListComponent` works. It loads the user's notes from the `NoteService` when the component initializes and also contains `select()` and `delete()` methods. It can talk to your secured Spring Boot API because the aforementioned `AuthInterceptor` adds an access token to the request.

Listing 66. src/app/note/note-list/note-list.component.ts

```
import { Component, OnInit } from '@angular/core';
import { NoteFilter } from '../note-filter';
import { NoteService } from '../note.service';
import { Note } from '../note';

@Component({
  selector: 'app-note',
  templateUrl: 'note-list.component.html'
})
export class NoteListComponent implements OnInit {
```

```
filter = new NoteFilter();
selectedNote!: Note;
feedback: any = {};

get noteList(): Note[] {
  return this.noteService.noteList;
}

constructor(private noteService: NoteService) {
}

ngOnInit() {
  this.search();
}

search(): void {
  this.noteService.load(this.filter);
}

select(selected: Note): void {
  this.selectedNote = selected;
}

delete(note: Note): void {
  if (confirm('Are you sure?')) {
    this.noteService.delete(note).subscribe({
      next: () => {
        this.feedback = {type: 'success', message: 'Delete was
successful!'};
        setTimeout(() => {
          this.search();
        }, 1000);
      },
      error: err => {
        this.feedback = {type: 'warning', message: 'Error deleting.'};
      }
    });
  }
}
}
}
```

The **Edit** link in this component's template links to the NoteEditComponent.

```
<a [routerLink]="['../notes', item.id ]" class="btn btn-secondary">Edit</a>
```

The NoteEditComponent has methods for loading a note, saving a note, and canceling.

```
import { Component, OnInit } from '@angular/core';
import { ActivatedRoute, Router } from '@angular/router';
import { NoteService } from '../note.service';
import { Note } from '../note';
import { map, switchMap } from 'rxjs/operators';
import { of } from 'rxjs';

@Component({
  selector: 'app-note-edit',
  templateUrl: './note-edit.component.html'
})
export class NoteEditComponent implements OnInit {

  id!: string;
  note!: Note;
  feedback: any = {};

  constructor(
    private route: ActivatedRoute,
    private router: Router,
    private noteService: NoteService) {
  }

  ngOnInit() {
    this
      .route
      .params
      .pipe(
        map(p => p['id']),
        switchMap(id => {
          if (id === 'new') { return of(new Note()); }
          return this.noteService.findById(id);
        })
      )
      .subscribe({
        next: note => {
          this.note = note;
          this.feedback = {};
        },
        error: err => {
          this.feedback = {type: 'warning', message: 'Error loading'};
        }
      });
  }

  save() {
    this.noteService.save(this.note).subscribe({
      next: note => {
        this.note = note;
        this.feedback = {type: 'success', message: 'Save was successful!'};
        setTimeout(async () => {
          await this.router.navigate(['/notes']);
```

```
        }, 1000);
      },
      error: err => {
        this.feedback = {type: 'warning', message: 'Error saving'};
      }
    });
  }

  async cancel() {
    await this.router.navigate(['/notes']);
  }
}
```

Fix the Note Edit Feature

One of the problems with the NoteEditComponent is it assumes the API returns an ID. Since Spring Data REST uses HATEOS by default, it returns links instead of IDs. You can change this default to return IDs by creating a RestConfiguration class in your Spring Boot app. You might notice you can also configure the base path in this class, instead of in application.properties.

Listing 67. notes-api/src/main/kotlin/com/okta/developer/notes/RestConfiguration.kt

```
package com.okta.developer.notes

import org.springframework.context.annotation.Configuration
import org.springframework.data.rest.core.config.RepositoryRestConfiguration
import org.springframework.data.rest.webmvc.config.RepositoryRestConfigurer
import org.springframework.web.servlet.config.annotation.CorsRegistry

@Configuration
class RestConfiguration : RepositoryRestConfigurer {

    override fun configureRepositoryRestConfiguration(
        config: RepositoryRestConfiguration?,
        cors: CorsRegistry?
    ) {
        config?.exposeIdsFor(Note::class.java)
        config?.setBasePath("/api")
    }
}
```

Another option is to modify the Angular side of things. Since the ID is passed into the NoteEditComponent, you can set it as a local variable, then set it on the note after it's returned. Here's a diff of what changes need to be made in notes/src/app/note/note-edit/note-edit.component.ts.

```
--- a/note/note-edit/note-edit.component.ts
+++ b/note/note-edit/note-edit.component.ts
@@ -29,12 +29,14 @@ export class NoteEditComponent implements OnInit {
        map(p => p['id']),
        switchMap(id => {
          if (id === 'new') { return of(new Note()); }
+         this.id = id;
          return this.noteService.findById(id);
        })
      )
      .subscribe({
        next: note => {
          this.note = note;
+         this.note.id = +note.id
          this.feedback = {};
        },
        error: err => {
@@ -47,6 +49,7 @@ export class NoteEditComponent implements OnInit {
      this.noteService.save(this.note).subscribe({
        next: note => {
          this.note = note;
+         this.note.id = +this.id;
          this.feedback = {type: 'success', message: 'Save was successful!'};
          setTimeout(async () => {
            await this.router.navigate(['/notes']);
```

In this example, you might notice this.note.id = +note.id. The + converts the string parameter to a number.

In the final example for this chapter, I opted to return IDs from my Spring Boot API.

Mocking Spring Security's OIDC Configuration

If you open a new terminal window and run ./gradlew test in the notes-api directory, tests will fail. This happens because Spring Security cannot connect to an identity provider on startup. You can run source .okta.env before running ./gradlew test to solve the problem. However, this is not a good long-term solution, especially for continuous integration.

To solve this problem, mock the OIDC configuration by creating a notes-api/src/test/···/notes/MockSecurityConfiguration.kt class.

Listing 68. notes-
api/src/test/kotlin/com/okta/developer/notes/MockSecurityConfiguration.kt

```kotlin
package com.okta.developer.notes

...

@TestConfiguration
class MockSecurityConfiguration {
    private val clientRegistration: ClientRegistration

    @Bean
    fun clientRegistrationRepository(): ClientRegistrationRepository {
        return InMemoryClientRegistrationRepository(clientRegistration)
    }

    private fun clientRegistration(): ClientRegistration.Builder {
        val metadata: MutableMap<String, Any> = HashMap()
        metadata["end_session_endpoint"] = "https://angular.org/logout"
        return ClientRegistration.withRegistrationId("okta")
            .redirectUri("{baseUrl}/{action}/oauth2/code/{registrationId}")
            .clientAuthenticationMethod(CLIENT_SECRET_BASIC)
            .authorizationGrantType(AUTHORIZATION_CODE)
            .scope("read:user")
            .authorizationUri("https://angular.org/login/oauth/authorize")
            .tokenUri("https://angular.org/login/oauth/access_token")
            .jwkSetUri("https://angular.org/oauth/jwk")
            .userInfoUri("https://api.angular.org/user")
            .providerConfigurationMetadata(metadata)
            .userNameAttributeName("id")
            .clientName("Client Name")
            .clientId("client-id")
            .clientSecret("client-secret")
    }

    @Bean
    fun jwtDecoder(): JwtDecoder {
        return mock(JwtDecoder::class.java)
    }

    @Bean
    fun authorizedService(registration: ClientRegistrationRepository?):
        OAuth2AuthorizedClientService {
        return InMemoryOAuth2AuthorizedClientService(registration)
    }

    @Bean
    fun authorizedRepository(client: OAuth2AuthorizedClientService?):
        OAuth2AuthorizedClientRepository {
        return AuthenticatedPrincipalOAuth2AuthorizedClientRepository(client)
    }
```

```
    init {
        clientRegistration = clientRegistration().build()
    }
}
```

Then, modify DemoApplicationTests.kt to use this class.

Listing 69. notes-api/src/test/kotlin/com/okta/developer/notes/DemoApplicationTests.kt

```
package com.okta.developer.notes

import org.junit.jupiter.api.Test
import org.springframework.boot.test.context.SpringBootTest

@SpringBootTest(classes = [DemoApplication::class,
MockSecurityConfiguration::class])
class DemoApplicationTests {

    @Test
    fun contextLoads() {
    }

}
```

Now, running ./gradlew test should pass as expected.

Summary

In this chapter, I showed you how to create Angular and Spring Boot apps and secure communication between them with OAuth 2.0 and OIDC. You used Kotlin on the back end; a language loved by many. You used Angular Schematics to generate code for authentication and CRUD, improving your efficiency as a developer.

This section did not show you how to make your Angular app look good, add validation, or how to deploy it to a public server. I'll tackle those topics in the next section.

 You can download the code for this book's examples from InfoQ. The angular-spring-boot directory has this chapter's completed example.

PART THREE

Beautiful Angular Apps with Bootstrap

I've been a fan of CSS frameworks since 2005. I led an open-source project called AppFuse at the time and wanted a way to provide themes for our users. We used Mike Stenhouse's CSS Framework and held a design contest to gather some themes we liked for our users. A couple of other CSS frameworks came along in the next few years, namely Blueprint in 2007 and Compass in 2008.

However, no CSS frameworks took the world by storm like Bootstrap. Back then, it was called Twitter Bootstrap. Mark Otto and Jacob Thornton invented it in mid-2010 while they worked at Twitter. As they wrote in "Building Twitter Bootstrap" in Issue 324 of *A List Apart*:

> Our goal is to provide a refined, well-documented, and extensive library of flexible design components built with HTML, CSS, and JavaScript for others to build and innovate on.

They released Bootstrap on August 19, 2011, and it quickly became *the* most popular project on GitHub. Developers like myself all over the world started using it. Bootstrap differed from previous CSS frameworks because it embraced mobile-first design and made responsiveness the norm for web design. Before Bootstrap, we built UIs for mobile apps with specialized frameworks like jQuery Mobile [https://jquerymobile.com/].

Another web framework took the world by storm the following year: AngularJS. AngularJS (v0.9) first appeared on GitHub in October 2010. The creators released version 1.0 on June 14, 2012.

Together, these frameworks have had quite a run. It's hard to believe they've lasted so long, especially considering both projects have had major rewrites!

I've heard many developers say that Angular is dead. As a veteran Java developer, I've heard this said about Java many times over the years as well. Yet it continues to thrive. Angular is similar in that it's become somewhat boring. Some people call boring frameworks "legacy." Others call them "revenue-generating."

Whatever you want to call it, Angular is far from dead.

Figure 26. Build Beautiful Angular Apps with Bootstrap

Angular Loves Bootstrap

You might think that Angular Material is more popular than Bootstrap these days. You may be right, but who you follow on Twitter shapes your popularity perspective. Bootstrap and Angular Material were quite popular among the fabulous folks that answered my recent poll. In 2019; 53% answered Bootstrap, and 33% answered Angular Material.

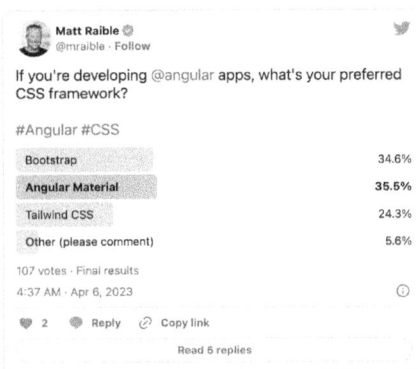

Figure 27. What's your preferred CSS framework with Angular?

Integrate Bootstrap with Angular

Integrating Bootstrap into an Angular application is fairly easy, thanks to NG Bootstrap. I'll start with the note-taking example from the last section. If you follow along, you'll convert the app to use Sass (because CSS is more fun with Sass), make the app look good, add form validation, and write some code to develop a searchable, sortable, and pageable data table. The last part sounds complex, but it only requires < 10 lines of code on the Spring Boot side of things. Kotlin and Spring Data JPA—FTW!

If you're following along, you should have an angular-spring-boot directory containing an Angular and a Spring Boot app.

If you'd rather start from this point, download the examples for this book from InfoQ. The angular-spring-boot directory has the previous section's completed example. Copy it to angular-bootstrap in your favorite code location.

Navigate into this new directory and its notes folder in a terminal. Then install the dependencies for the Angular app.

```
cd angular-bootstrap/notes
npm install
```

Add Bootstrap and NG Bootstrap:

```
rm package-lock.json
ng update @angular/cli @angular/core
ng add @ng-bootstrap/ng-bootstrap@14
```

This process will import NgbModule in app.module.ts and configure your app to use Bootstrap by adding a reference to bootstrap.min.css in angular.json.

If you run ng serve -o, you'll see it's pretty simple. And kinda ugly.

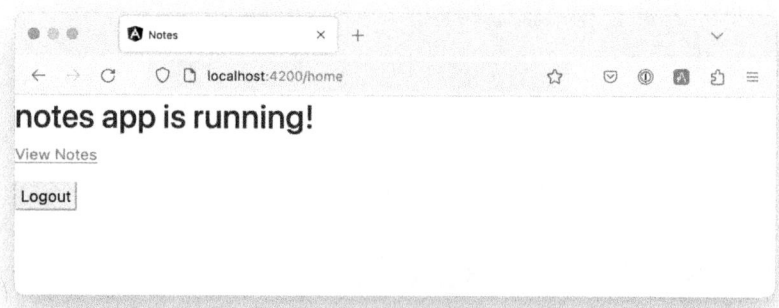

Figure 28. Bare-bones styling

Let's fix that!

Security Configuration

Both apps should have their security configured to use OIDC from the last chapter. If you need to register apps for them, you can use the Auth0 CLI.

```
auth0 apps create \
  --name "Angular" \
  --description "Angular OIDC App" \
  --type spa \
  --callbacks http://localhost:4200/home \
  --logout-urls http://localhost:4200 \
  --origins http://localhost:4200 \
  --web-origins http://localhost:4200

# Copy your domain and client ID into notes/src/app/auth-
routing.module.ts

auth0 apps create \
  --name "Spring Boot" \
  --description "Spring Boot OIDC App" \
  --type regular \
  --callbacks http://localhost:8080/login/oauth2/code/okta \
  --logout-urls http://localhost:8080 \
  --reveal-secrets

# Copy the results of this command into notes-api/.okta.env or
# copy .okta.env from the angular-spring-boot project and
# update the client ID and secret.
```

Restart each app:

```
# in the notes directory
npm start

# in the notes-api directory
source .okta.env
./gradlew bootRun
```

Begin by changing app.component.html to use Bootstrap classes.

Listing 70. src/app/app.component.html

```
<nav class="navbar navbar-expand-lg navbar-dark bg-dark">
```

```
  <div class="container-fluid">
    <a class="navbar-brand text-light" href="#">{{ title }} app is
running!</a>
  </div>
</nav>

<div class="container-fluid pt-3">
  <router-outlet></router-outlet>
</div>
```

Now we're getting somewhere!

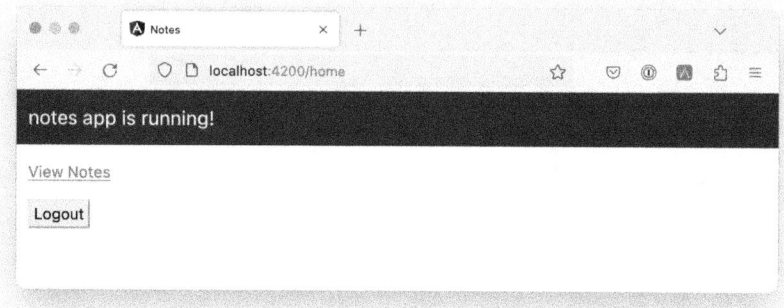

Figure 29. Slightly styled

Enter a note, and you'll see it in the list.

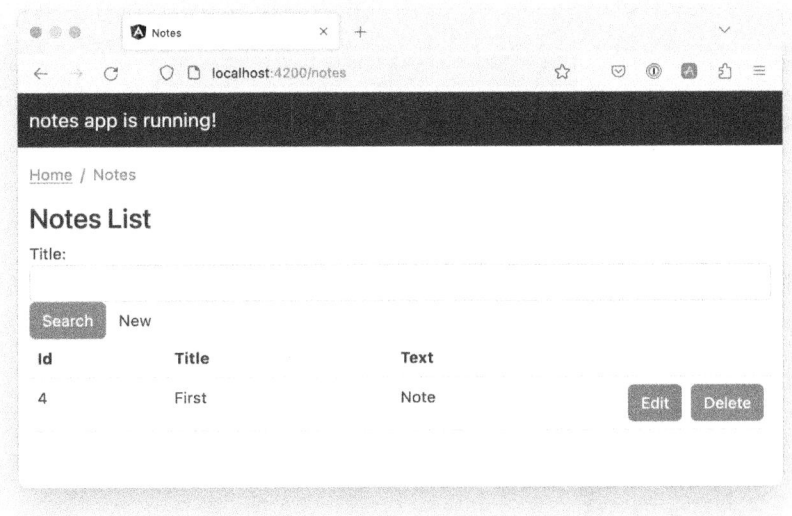

Figure 30. First note

You'll notice it looks *pretty good*, but things aren't quite *beautiful*. Yet...

Use Sass to Customize Bootstrap

Before you make things awesome, I'd like to show you how to convert from CSS with Angular to Sass. Why? Because Sass [https://sass-lang.com/] is completely compatible with CSS, and it makes CSS more like programming. It also allows you to customize Bootstrap by overriding its variables.

 If you're not into Sass, you can skip this section. Everything will still work without it.

If you run the following find command in the notes project...

```
find . -name "*.css" -not -path "./node_modules/*"
```

...you'll see three files have a .css extension.

```
./src/app/home/home.component.css
./src/app/app.component.css
./src/styles.css
```

You can manually rename these to have a .scss extension or do it programmatically.

```
find . -name "*.css" -not -path "./node_modules/*" | rename -v "s/css/scss/g"
```

 I had to brew install rename on my Mac for this command to work.

Then, replace all references to .css files.

```
find ./src/app -type f -exec sed -i '' -e 's/.css/.scss/g' {} \;
```

Modify angular.json to reference src/styles.scss (in the build and test sections) and remove bootstrap.min.css.

```
"styles": [
  "src/styles.scss"
],
```

And change styles.scss to import Bootstrap's Sass.

Listing 71. src/styles.scss

```
@import 'bootstrap/scss/bootstrap.scss';
```

To demonstrate how to override Bootstrap's variables, create a src/_variables.scss and override the colors. You can see the default variables in Bootstrap's GitHub repo [https://github.com/twbs/bootstrap/blob/v5.2.3/scss/_variables.scss].

```
$primary: orange;
$secondary: blue;
$light: lighten($primary, 20%);
$dark: darken($secondary, 10%);
```

Then import this file at the top of src/styles.scss:

```
@import 'variables', 'bootstrap/scss/bootstrap.scss';
```

You'll see the colors change after these updates.

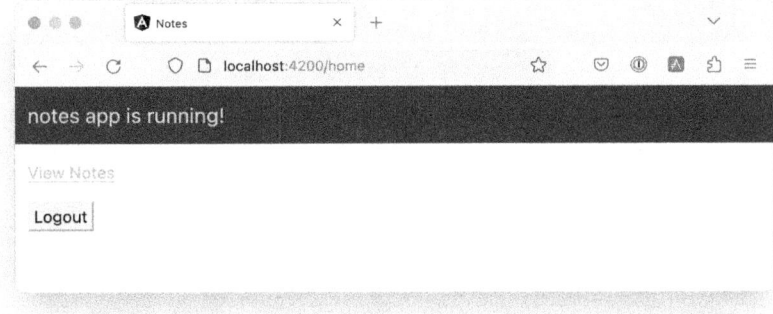

Figure 31. Customized Bootstrap variables

Comment out (or remove) the variables in _variables.scss to revert to Bootstrap's default colors.

Make Your Angular App Beautiful with Bootstrap

You can see from the screenshots above that angular-crud generates screens with some styling, but it's not quite right. Let's add a Navbar in app.component.html. Change its HTML to have a collapsible navbar (for mobile devices), add links to useful sites, and add login/logout buttons. While you're at it, display a message to the user when they aren't authenticated.

Listing 72. src/app/app.component.html

```
<nav class="navbar navbar-expand-lg navbar-dark bg-dark">
  <div class="container-fluid">
    <a class="navbar-brand" href="#">
      <img src="/assets/images/angular.svg" width="30" height="30"
          class="d-inline-block align-top" alt="Angular">
      {{ title }}
    </a>
    <button class="navbar-toggler" type="button" data-toggle="collapse"
          data-target="#navbarSupportedContent" aria-
controls="navbarSupportedContent"
          aria-expanded="false" aria-label="Toggle navigation">
      <span class="navbar-toggler-icon"></span>
    </button>
```

```
<div class="collapse navbar-collapse" id="navbarSupportedContent">
  <ul class="navbar-nav ms-auto mb-2 mb-lg-0">
    <li class="nav-item">
      <a class="nav-link" href="#">Home</a>
    </li>
    <li class="nav-item">
      <a class="nav-link" href="https://twitter.com/mraible">@mraible</a>
    </li>
    <li class="nav-item">
      <a class="nav-link" href="https://github.com/mraible">GitHub</a>
    </li>
  </ul>
  <form class="d-flex">
    <button *ngIf="(auth.isAuthenticated$ | async) === false"
            (click)="login()" type="button"
            class="btn btn-outline-primary">Login</button>
    <button *ngIf="auth.isAuthenticated$ | async"
            (click)="logout()" type="button"
            class="btn btn-outline-secondary">Logout</button>
  </form>
</div>
  </div>
</nav>

<div class="container-fluid pt-3">
  <a *ngIf="(auth.isAuthenticated$ | async) === false">Please log in to
manage your notes.</a>
  <router-outlet></router-outlet>
</div>
```

Download the angular.svg file from angular.io/presskit and add it to your project. You can do this quickly by running the following command from the notes directory.

```
wget https://angular.io/assets/images/logos/angular/angular.svg -P
src/assets/images/
```

Add AuthService and DOCUMENT as imports to AppComponent, inject them into the constructor, and add login() and logout() methods.

```
import { Component, Inject } from '@angular/core';
import { AuthService } from '@auth0/auth0-angular';
import { DOCUMENT } from '@angular/common';

@Component({
  selector: 'app-root',
  templateUrl: './app.component.html',
  styleUrls: ['./app.component.scss']
})
```

```
export class AppComponent {
  title = 'notes';

  constructor(public auth: AuthService, @Inject(DOCUMENT) private doc:
Document) {
  }

  login(): void {
    this.auth.loginWithRedirect();
  }

  logout(): void {
    this.auth.logout({
      logoutParams: {
        returnTo: this.doc.location.origin
      }
    });
  }
}
```

Remove the login and logout buttons from home.component.html:

Listing 73. src/app/home/home.component.html

```
<p><a routerLink="/notes" *ngIf="auth.isAuthenticated$ | async">View
Notes</a></p>
```

You can also remove the login() and logout() methods from
home.component.ts.

Listing 74. src/app/home/home.component.ts

```
import { Component, Inject } from '@angular/core';
import { AuthService } from '@auth0/auth0-angular';

@Component({
  selector: 'app-home',
  templateUrl: './home.component.html',
  styleUrls: ['./home.component.scss']
})
export class HomeComponent {

  constructor(public auth: AuthService) {
  }
}
```

Run ng serve and you'll be able to see your stylish app at
http://localhost:4200.

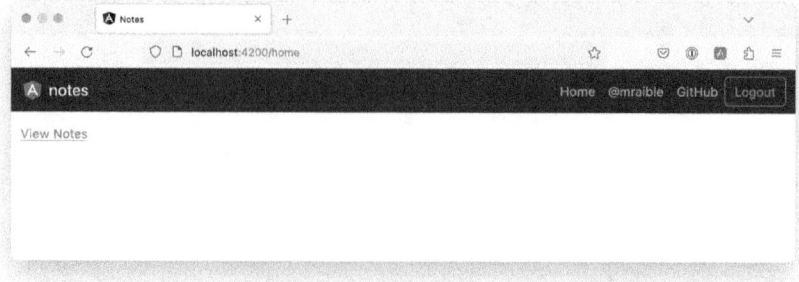

Figure 32. Notes app with navbar

Fix Bootstrap's Responsive Menu

If you reduce the width of your browser window, you'll see the menu collapse to take up less real estate.

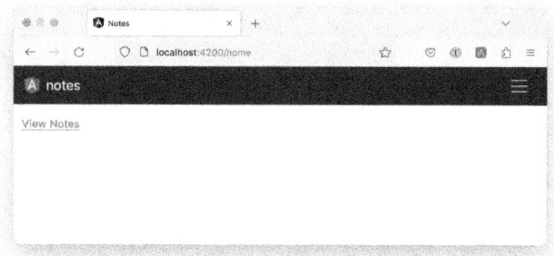

Figure 33. Navbar squished

However, if you click on it, the menu doesn't expand. To fix that, you must use the ngbCollapse directive from NG Bootstrap. Modify app.component.html to have a click handler on the navbar toggle and add ngbCollapse to the menu.

Listing 75. src/app/app/app.component.html

```
<button (click)="isCollapsed = !isCollapsed" class="navbar-toggler" ...>
  ...
</button>

<div [ngbCollapse]="isCollapsed" class="collapse navbar-collapse" ...>
  ...
</div>
```

Then add isCollapsed in app.component.ts and change the title to be capitalized.

Listing 76. src/app/app/app.component.ts

```
export class AppComponent {
  title = 'Notes';
  isCollapsed = true;

  ...

}
```

Now, you'll be able to toggle the menu!

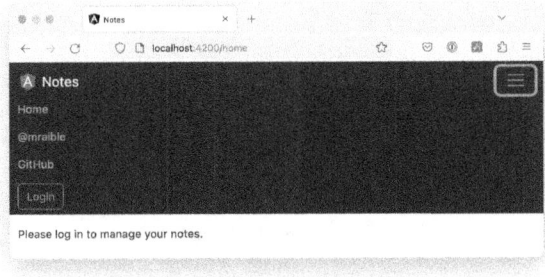

Figure 34. Squished navbar with menu

Refactor Unit Tests to Pass

You changed some elements and values that will cause tests in app.component.spec.ts to fail. Update the tests to look for uppercase "Note" and import NgbModule.

Listing 77. src/app/app.component.spec.ts

```
import { NgbModule } from '@ng-bootstrap/ng-bootstrap';

describe('AppComponent', () => {
  ...

  beforeEach(waitForAsync(() => {
    TestBed.configureTestingModule({
      imports: [
        ...
        NgbModule
      ],
      ...
    }).compileComponents();
```

```
    }));

    ...

    it(`should have as title 'notes'`, () => {
      const fixture = TestBed.createComponent(AppComponent);
      const app = fixture.componentInstance;
      expect(app.title).toEqual('Notes');
    });

    it('should render title', () => {
      const fixture = TestBed.createComponent(AppComponent);
      fixture.detectChanges();
      const compiled = fixture.nativeElement as HTMLElement;
      expect(compiled.querySelector('nav')?.textContent).toContain('Notes');
    });
  });
```

Update the Note List Angular Template

Modify the note-list.component.html so the search form is all on one line.

Listing 78. src/app/note/note-list/note-list.component.html

```
...
<h2>Notes List</h2>
<form #f="ngForm" class="row g-2">
  <div class="col-auto">
    <input [(ngModel)]="filter.title" type="search" name="query"
           placeholder="Title" class="form-control ml-2 mr-2">
  </div>
  <div class="col-auto">
    <button (click)="search($event)" [disabled]="!f?.valid"
            class="btn btn-primary">Search</button>
    <a [routerLink]="['../notes', 'new' ]"
            class="btn btn-default ml-2">New</a>
  </div>
</form>
...
```

That looks better!

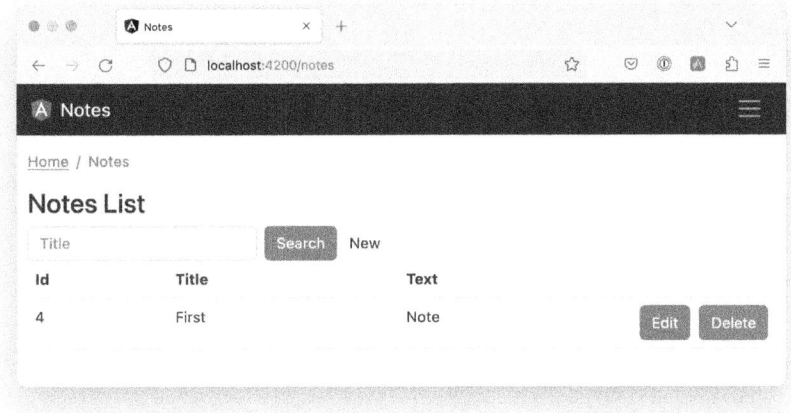

Figure 35. Styled Notes List

Add Validation and Bootstrap to the Note Edit Template

If you click the **New** button, you'll see the form needs some work, too. Bootstrap has excellent support for stylish forms using its `form-label` and `form-control` classes. `note-edit.component.html` already uses these classes, but there are updates needed for Bootstrap 5.

The following HTML will add floating labels to your form using the `form-floating` class and add more spacing with `mb-3`.

Listing 79. src/app/note/note-edit/note-edit.component.html

```
<nav aria-label="breadcrumb">
  <ol class="breadcrumb">
    <li class="breadcrumb-item"><a routerLink="/">Home</a></li>
    <li class="breadcrumb-item active">Notes</li>
  </ol>
</nav>
<h2>Notes Detail</h2>
<div *ngIf="feedback.message"
     class="alert alert-{{feedback.type}}">{{ feedback.message }}</div>
<form *ngIf="note" #editForm="ngForm" (ngSubmit)="save()"
      class="form-floating">

  <div class="mb-3">
    <label>Id</label>
    {{note.id || 'n/a'}}
  </div>

  <div class="form-floating mb-3">
    <input [(ngModel)]="note.title" id="title" name="title"
```

```
                  class="form-control" placeholder="title">
      <label for="title">Title</label>
   </div>

   <div class="form-floating mb-3">
      <input [(ngModel)]="note.text" id="text" name="text"
             class="form-control" placeholder="text">
      <label for="text">Text</label>
   </div>

   <div class="btn-group mt-3" role="group">
      <button type="submit" class="btn btn-primary"
              [disabled]="!editForm.form.valid">Save</button>
      <button type="button" class="btn btn-secondary ml-2"
              (click)="cancel()">Cancel</button>
   </div>
 </form>
```

That's an improvement!

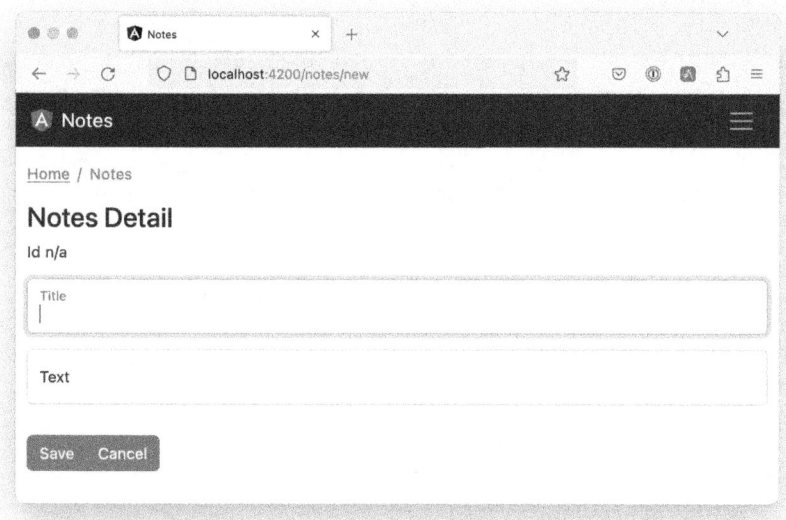

Figure 36. Styled Notes Form

To make the title field required, add a required attribute to its <input> tag, along with a name so that it can be referenced in an error message.

```
<div class="form-floating mb-3">
  <input [(ngModel)]="note.title" id="title" name="title" #name="ngModel"
         class="form-control" placeholder="title" required
         [ngClass]="{'is-invalid': name.touched && name.invalid,
                     'is-valid': name.touched && name.valid}">
  <div [hidden]="name.valid" style="display: block" class="invalid-feedback">
    Title is required
  </div>
  <label for="title">Title</label>
</div>
```

You might notice the expression on the [ngClass] attribute. This adds CSS classes to the element as validation rules pass and fail. It's a cool feature that web developers love!

When you add a new note, it'll let you know it requires a title.

Figure 37. Title is required

If you give it focus and leave, it'll add a red border around the field.

Figure 38. Dirty title validation decoration

Add a Data Table with Searching, Sorting, and Pagination

At the beginning of this section, I said I'd show you how to develop a searchable, sortable, and pageable data table. NG Bootstrap has a complete example [https://ng-bootstrap.github.io/#/components/table/examples] I used to build the section below. The major difference is you'll be using a real server, not a simulated one. Spring Data JPA has some slick features that make this possible, namely its query methods and paging/sorting.

Add Search by Title with Spring Data JPA

Adding search functionality requires the fewest code modifications. Change the `UserController#notes()` method in your Spring Boot app to accept a title parameter and return notes with the parameter's value in their title.

Listing 80. notes-api/src/main/kotlin/.../notes/UserController.kt

```
@GetMapping("/user/notes")
fun notes(principal: Principal, title: String?): List<Note> {
    println("Fetching notes for user: ${principal.name}")
    return if (title.isNullOrEmpty()) {
        repository.findAllByUsername(principal.name)
    } else {
        println("Searching for title: ${title}")

repository.findAllByUsernameAndTitleContainingIgnoreCase(principal.name,
title)
    }
}
```

Add the new repository method to the `NotesRepository` in `DemoApplication.kt`.

Listing 81. notes-api/src/main/kotlin/.../notes/DemoApplication.kt

```
@RepositoryRestResource
interface NotesRepository : JpaRepository<Note, Long> {
    fun findAllByUsername(name: String): List<Note>
    fun findAllByUsernameAndTitleContainingIgnoreCase(name: String, term:
String): List<Note>
}
```

Restart your server and add a few notes, and you should be able to search for them by title in your Angular app. I love how Spring Data JPA makes this so easy!

Add Sort Functionality with Angular and Bootstrap

To begin, create a `sortable.directive.ts` directive to show a direction indicator.

Listing 82. src/app/note/note-list/sortable.directive.ts

```
import { Directive, EventEmitter, Input, Output } from '@angular/core';

export type SortDirection = 'asc' | 'desc' | '';
const rotate: { [key: string]: SortDirection } = {asc: 'desc', desc: '', '':
'asc'};

export interface SortEvent {
```

```
    column: string;
    direction: SortDirection;
}

@Directive({
  selector: 'th[sortable]',
  host: {
    '[class.asc]': 'direction === "asc"',
    '[class.desc]': 'direction === "desc"',
    '(click)': 'rotate()'
  }
})
export class SortableHeaderDirective {

  @Input() sortable!: string;
  @Input() direction: SortDirection = '';
  @Output() sort = new EventEmitter<SortEvent>();

  rotate() {
    this.direction = rotate[this.direction];
    this.sort.emit({column: this.sortable, direction: this.direction});
  }
}
```

Add it as a declaration in note.module.ts.

Listing 83. src/app/note/note.module.ts

```
import { SortableHeaderDirective } from './note-list/sortable.directive';

@NgModule({
  ...
  declarations: [
    ...
    SortableHeaderDirective
  ],
  ...
}
```

Add a headers variable to note-list.component.ts and an onSort() method.

Listing 84. src/app/note/note-list/note-list.component.ts

```
import { Component, OnInit, QueryList, ViewChildren } from '@angular/core';
import { SortableHeaderDirective, SortEvent } from './sortable.directive';

export class NoteListComponent implements OnInit {
  @ViewChildren(SortableHeaderDirective) headers!:
QueryList<SortableHeaderDirective>;
```

```
    ...

    onSort({column, direction}: SortEvent) {
      // reset other headers
      this.headers.forEach(header => {
        if (header.sortable !== column) {
          header.direction = '';
        }
      });

      this.filter.column = column;
      this.filter.direction = direction;
      this.search();
    }

    ...
  }
```

Update the `note-filter.ts` to have `column` and `direction` properties.

Listing 85. src/app/note/note-filter.ts

```
export class NoteFilter {
  title = '';
  column!: string;
  direction!: string;
}
```

Modify the `find()` method in `NoteService` to pass a sort parameter when appropriate.

Listing 86. src/app/note/note.service.ts

```
import { map } from 'rxjs/operators';

...

find(filter: NoteFilter): Observable<Note[]> {
  const params: any = {
    title: filter.title,
    sort: `${filter.column},${filter.direction}`,
  };
  if (!filter.direction) { delete params.sort; }

  const userNotes = 'http://localhost:8080/user/notes';
  return this.http.get(userNotes, {params, headers}).pipe(
    map((response: any) => {
      return response.content;
    })
  );
```

```
}
```

Update note-list.component.html so it uses the sortable directive and calls onSort() when a user clicks it.

Listing 87. src/app/note/note-list/note-list.component.html

```
<thead>
  <tr>
    <th class="border-top-0" scope="col">#</th>
    <th class="border-top-0" scope="col" sortable="title"
        (sort)="onSort($event)">Title</th>
    <th class="border-top-0" scope="col" sortable="text"
        (sort)="onSort($event)">Text</th>
    <th class="border-top-0" scope="col" style="width:120px"></th>
  </tr>
</thead>
```

Add CSS in styles.scss to show a sort indicator when a user sorts a column.

Listing 88. src/styles.scss

```
th[sortable] {
  cursor: pointer;
  user-select: none;
  -webkit-user-select: none;
}

th[sortable].desc:before, th[sortable].asc:before {
  content: '';
  display: block;
  background:
url('data:image/png;base64,iVBORw0KGgoAAAANSUhEUgAAAAEAAAABACAYAAACqaXHeAAAAAX
NSR0IArs4c6QAAAAmxJREFUeAHtmksrRVEUx72fH8CIGQNJkpGUUmakDEiZSJRIZsRQmCkTJRmZmJg
QE0kpX0D5DJKJgff7v+ru2u3O3vvc67TOvsdatdrnnP1Y///v7HvvubdbUiIhBISAEBACQkAICAEh
IAQ4CXSh2DnyDfmCPEG2Iv9F9F9MP1M/LHyAecdyMzHYNwNwR3fdNK/OH9HXl1UCozD24TCvILxizEDWI
EzA0FcM8woCgRrJCoS5SP1wrANQSMAJX1LEI9bqpQo4JYNFFKRSvIgsxHDVnqZgIkPnNBM0rIGtYk9
YOOsqqbgepRCfdbmFtqhFkVEDVPjJp0+Z6e6hRHhqBKgg6ZDCvYBygVmUoEGoh5JTRvIJwhJo1aUO
oh4CLPMyvvxxi7EWOMgnCGsXXI1GIXlZUYX7ucU+kbR8NW81h3O7cue0Pk32MKKndfUxQFAwxdirk3f
HappAnc0oqDPzDfGTBrCfHP04dM4oTV8cxr0SVzH9FF07xD3ib6xCDE+M+aUcVygtWzzbtGX2rPBr
EUYfecfQkaFzYi6HjVnGBdtL7epqAlc1+jRdAap74RrnPc4BCijttY2tRcdN0g17w7HqZrXhdJTYA
uS3hd8z+vKgK3V1zWPae0mZDMykadBn1hTQBLnZNwVrJpSe/NwEeDsEwCctEOsJTsgxLvCqUl2ACf
tEGvJDgjxrnBqkh3ASTvEWrIDQrwrnJpkB3DSDrGW7IAQ7wqnJtkB3ASEhIAQYCLwC8Jxp
AmsEGt6AAAAAElFTkSuQmCC') no-repeat;
  background-size: 22px;
  width: 22px;
  height: 22px;
  float: left;
  margin-left: -22px;
```

```
}

th[sortable].desc:before {
  transform: rotate(180deg);
  -ms-transform: rotate(180deg);
}
```

Add Sorting and Paging in Spring Boot with Spring Data JPA

On the server, you can use Spring Data's support for paging and sorting.
Add a Pageable argument to UserController#notes() and return a Page
instead of a List.

Listing 89. notes-api/src/main/kotlin/.../notes/UserController.kt

```
package com.okta.developer.notes

import org.springframework.data.domain.Page
import org.springframework.data.domain.Pageable
import org.springframework.security.core.annotation.AuthenticationPrincipal
import org.springframework.security.oauth2.core.oidc.user.OidcUser
import org.springframework.web.bind.annotation.GetMapping
import org.springframework.web.bind.annotation.RestController
import java.security.Principal

@RestController
class UserController(val repository: NotesRepository) {

    @GetMapping("/user/notes")
    fun notes(principal: Principal, title: String?, pageable: Pageable):
Page<Note> {
        println("Fetching notes for user: ${principal.name}")
        return if (title.isNullOrEmpty()) {
            repository.findAllByUsername(principal.name, pageable)
        } else {
            println("Searching for title: ${title}")

repository.findAllByUsernameAndTitleContainingIgnoreCase(principal.name,
title, pageable)
        }
    }

    @GetMapping("/user")
    fun user(@AuthenticationPrincipal user: OidcUser): OidcUser {
        return user
    }
}
```

Modify NotesRepository to add a Pageable argument to its methods and return a Page.

Listing 90. notes-api/src/main/kotlin/.../notes/DemoApplication.kt

```
import org.springframework.data.domain.Page
import org.springframework.data.domain.Pageable

...

@RepositoryRestResource
interface NotesRepository : JpaRepository<Note, Long> {
    fun findAllByUsername(name: String, pageable: Pageable): Page<Note>
    fun findAllByUsernameAndTitleContainingIgnoreCase(name: String, term:
String, pageable: Pageable): Page<Note>
}
```

While you're updating the Spring Boot side of things, modify DataInitializer to create a thousand notes for your user.

Listing 91. notes-api/src/main/kotlin/.../notes/DataInitializer.kt

```
@Component
class DataInitializer(val repository: NotesRepository) : ApplicationRunner {

    @Throws(Exception::class)
    override fun run(args: ApplicationArguments) {
        for (x in 0..1000) {
            repository.save(Note(title = "Note ${x}", username = "<your
email>"))
        }
        repository.findAll().forEach { println(it) }
    }
}
```

Make sure to replace <your email> *with the email address you use to log in to Auth0.*

The principal.name will not default to the user's email address. To fix this, you need to add an Action in Auth0 that will add the email address to the access token. Log in to your Auth0 management dashboard and go to **Actions > Library > Build Custom**.

Name it "Add email claim" and click **Create**. Replace the code with the following:

```
exports.onExecutePostLogin = async (event, api) => {
```

```
  const namespace = 'https://angular-book.org';
  if (event.authorization) {
    api.accessToken.setCustomClaim(`${namespace}/email`, event.user.email);
  }
};
```

Select **Save Draft** and then **Deploy**.

Now go to **Actions** > **Flows** > **Login** and add the action to the flow from the **Custom** panel on the right. Click **Apply**. The results should look as follows:

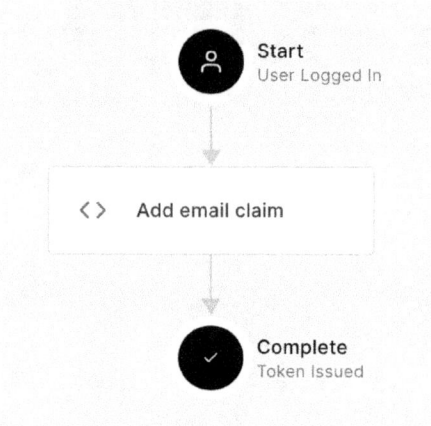

When you log in, the email address will be added to the access token.

Adjust the `UserController` to use the email address from the access token instead of the `principal.name`.

Listing 92. src/main/kotlin/com/okta/developer/notes/UserController.kt

```
@GetMapping("/user/notes")
fun notes(principal: Principal, title: String?, pageable: Pageable):
Page<Note> {
    val jwt: JwtAuthenticationToken = principal as JwtAuthenticationToken
    val email = jwt.tokenAttributes
        .getOrDefault("https://angular-book.org/email",
principal.name).toString()
    println("Fetching notes for user: ${email}")
    return if (title.isNullOrEmpty()) {
        repository.findAllByUsername(email, pageable)
    } else {
        println("Searching for title: ${title}")
        repository.findAllByUsernameAndTitleContainingIgnoreCase(email,
title, pageable)
    }
```

```
}
```

Modify the `AddUserToNote` class in `DemoApplication` too.

```
class AddUserToNote {

    @HandleBeforeCreate
    fun handleCreate(note: Note) {
        val auth = SecurityContextHolder.getContext().authentication
        val email = (auth as JwtAuthenticationToken).tokenAttributes
            .getOrDefault("https://angular-book.org/email",
auth.name).toString()
        note.username = email
        println("Creating note: $note")
    }
}
```

Restart your Spring Boot app to make the data available for searching. Click on the **Title** column to see sorting in action!

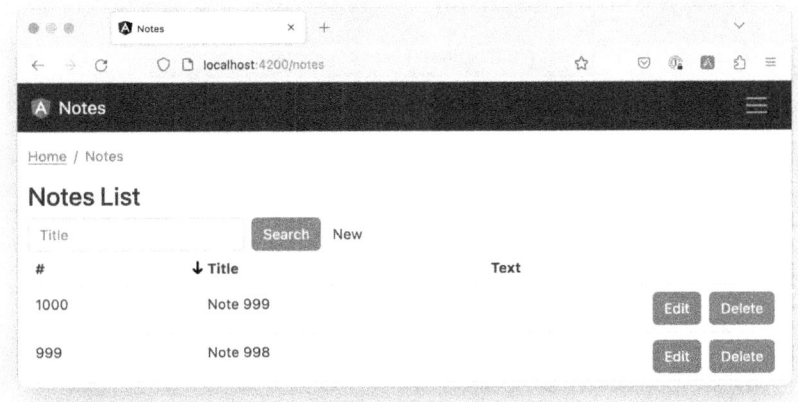

Figure 39. Notes list with sorting

Add Pagination with Angular and Bootstrap

The last feature to add is pagination with NG Bootstrap's `<ngb-pagination>` component. Begin by adding `page` and `size` variables (with default values) to `note-filter.ts`.

Listing 93. notes/src/app/note/note-filter.ts

```
export class NoteFilter {
```

```
  title = '';
  column!: string;
  direction!: string;
  page = 0;
  size = 20;
}
```

At the bottom of `note-list.component.html` (just after `</table>`), add the
pagination component, along with a page-size selector.

Listing 94. notes/src/app/note/note-list/note-list.component.html

```
<div class="d-flex justify-content-between p-2">
  <ngb-pagination [maxSize]="10" [collectionSize]="total$ | async"
                  [(page)]="filter.page" [pageSize]="filter.size"
                  (pageChange)="onPageChange(filter.page)">
  </ngb-pagination>

  <select class="custom-select" style="width: auto" name="pageSize"
          [(ngModel)]="filter.size" (ngModelChange)="onChange(filter.size)">
    <option [ngValue]="10">10 items per page</option>
    <option [ngValue]="20">20 items per page</option>
    <option [ngValue]="100">100 items per page</option>
  </select>
</div>
```

You might notice "total$ | async" in this code and wonder what it means.
This is an `async` pipe [https://angular.io/api/common/AsyncPipe] that subscribes to
an `Observable` or `Promise` and returns the last value produced. It's a handy
way to subscribe to real-time updates.

Add `NgbModule` as an import to `note.module.ts`.

Listing 95. src/app/note/note.module.ts

```
import { NgbModule } from '@ng-bootstrap/ng-bootstrap';

@NgModule({
  imports: [
    ...
    NgbModule
  ],
  ...
}
```

In `note-list.component.ts`, add a `total$` observable and set it from the
`search()` method. Then add an `onPageChange()` method and an `onChange()`

method, and modify onSort() to set the page to 0.

Listing 96. src/app/note/note-list/note-list.component.ts

```
import { Observable } from 'rxjs';

export class NoteListComponent implements OnInit {
  total$!: Observable<any>;

  ...

  search(event?: Event): void {
    if (event) {
      this.filter.page = 0;
    }
    this.noteService.load(this.filter);
    this.total$ = this.noteService.size$;
  }

  onChange(pageSize: number) {
    this.filter.size = pageSize;
    this.filter.page = 0;
    this.search();
  }

  onPageChange(page: number) {
    this.filter.page = page - 1;
    this.search();
    this.filter.page = page;
  }

  onSort({column, direction}: SortEvent) {
    // reset other headers
    this.headers.forEach(header => {
      if (header.sortable !== column) {
        header.direction = '';
      }
    });

    this.filter.column = column;
    this.filter.direction = direction;
    this.filter.page = 0;
    this.search();
  }
}
```

Then update notes.service.ts to add a size$ observable and parameters for the page size and page number.

Listing 97. src/app/note/note.service.ts

```
import { BehaviorSubject } from 'rxjs';

...

export class NoteService {
  ...
  size$ = new BehaviorSubject<number>(0);

  ...

  find(filter: NoteFilter): Observable<Note[]> {
    const params: any = {
      title: filter.title,
      sort: `${filter.column},${filter.direction}`,
      size: filter.size,
      page: filter.page
    };
    if (!filter.direction) { delete params.sort; }

    const userNotes = 'http://localhost:8080/user/notes';
    return this.http.get(userNotes, {params, headers}).pipe(
      map((response: any) => {
        this.size$.next(response.totalElements);
        return response.content;
      })
    );
  }

  ...
}
```

Now your note list should have a working pagination feature at the bottom. Pretty slick, eh?

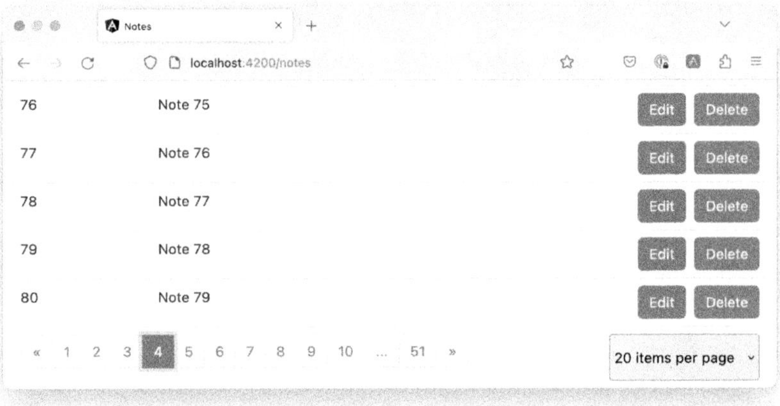

Figure 40. Notes with pagination

Angular + Bootstrap + Spring Boot = JHipster

Phew! That was a lot of code. I hope this section has helped you see how powerful Angular and Spring Boot with Bootstrap can be!

I also wanted to let you know you can get a lot of this functionality for free with JHipster [http://jhipster.tech]. It even has Kotlin support [https://github.com/jhipster/jhipster-kotlin]. You can generate a Notes CRUD app that uses Angular, Bootstrap, Spring Boot, and Kotlin in just three steps.

1. Install Node 16 for JHipster 7. If you're using nvm [https://github.com/nvm-sh/nvm], run `nvm use 16`.

2. Install JHipster and KHipster:

   ```
   npm install -g generator-jhipster generator-jhipster-kotlin
   ```

3. Create an easy-notes directory and a notes.jdl file in it:

   ```
   application {
     config {
       baseName notes
       authenticationType oauth2
       buildTool gradle
       searchEngine elasticsearch
       testFrameworks [cypress]
   ```

```
  }
  entities *
}
entity Note {
  title String required
  text TextBlob
}
relationship ManyToOne {
  Note{user(login)} to User
}
paginate Note with pagination
```

4. In a terminal, navigate to the easy-notes directory and run:

```
khipster jdl notes.jdl
```

That's it!

Of course, you probably want to see it running. Run the following commands to start Keycloak (as a local OAuth 2.0 server) and Elasticsearch, and launch the app.

```
docker-compose -f src/main/docker/keycloak.yml up -d
docker-compose -f src/main/docker/elasticsearch.yml up -d
./gradlew
```

Then, run npm run e2e in another terminal window to verify everything works. Here's a screenshot of the app's Notes form with validation.

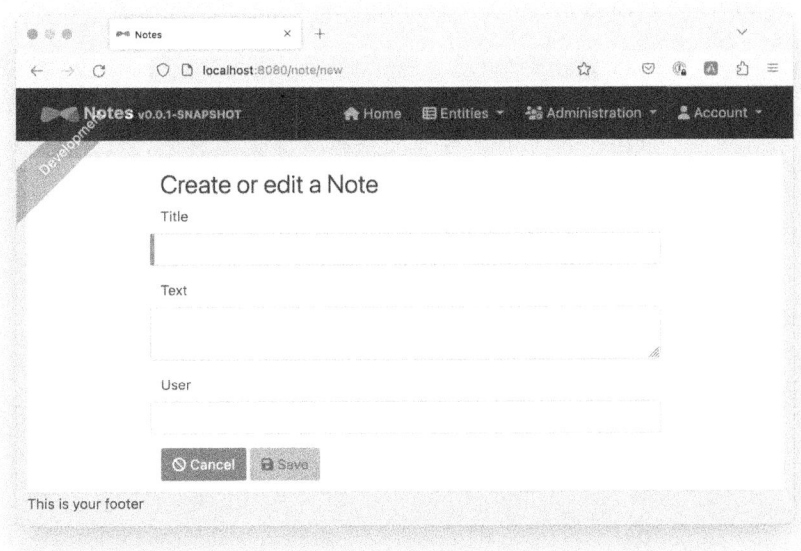

Figure 41. KHipster Notes

 Want to make JHipster work with Auth0? See JHipster's
security documentation [https://www.jhipster.tech/security/#
auth0].

Summary

In this chapter, I showed you how to use Bootstrap to make your Angular
app look good, configure form validation, and add a searchable, sortable,
and pageable data table feature.

I used the following resources to gather historical information about
Angular and Bootstrap.

- Refreshing AppFuse's UI with Twitter Bootstrap [https://raibledesigns.com/
  rd/entry/refreshing_appfuse_s_ui_with]

- Building Twitter Bootstrap [https://alistapart.com/article/building-twitter-
  bootstrap/]

- Bootstrap > About > History [https://getbootstrap.com/docs/4.0/about/history/]

- Angular 1.0 Turns Five Years Old [https://medium.com/dailyjs/angular-1-0-
  turns-five-years-old-4d7108a5e412]

In the next section, I'll show you how to deploy your Angular app to production. Buckle up!

 You can download the code for this book's examples from InfoQ. The `angular-bootstrap` directory has this chapter's completed example.

PART
FOUR

Angular Deployment

One of the more popular combinations of front-end and back-end frameworks is Angular + Spring Boot. Combining the two is possible—from keeping them as separate apps to combining them into a single artifact. But what about deployment?

Developers ask me from time to time, "What's the best way to do Angular deployment?" In this section, I'll show you several options. I'll start by showing you how to deploy a Spring Boot app to Heroku. Then, I'll show how to deploy a separate Angular app to Heroku.

There are many tutorials and information in the Java community on how to deploy Spring Boot apps, so I'll leave the Spring Boot API on Heroku and show other Angular deployment options, including Firebase, Netlify, and AWS S3.

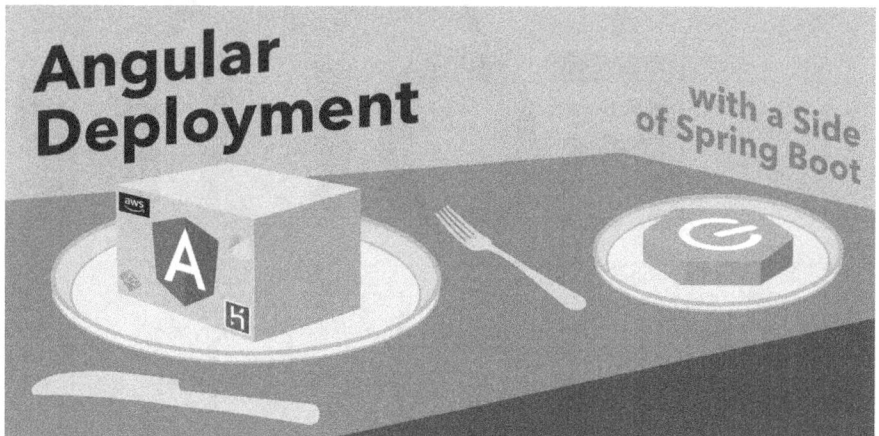

Figure 42. Angular Deployment with a Side of Spring Boot

Create an Angular + Spring Boot App

If you're following along, you should have an angular-bootstrap directory with an Angular and a Spring Boot app in it. It's a note-taking app that uses Kotlin and Spring Boot on the back end and Angular on the front end. It's secured with OpenID Connect (OIDC).

If you'd rather start from this point, download the examples for this book from InfoQ. The angular-bootstrap directory has the previous section's completed example. Copy it to angular-deployment in your favorite code location.

One of the slick features of this app is its full-featured data table that allows sorting, searching, and pagination. This feature is powered by NG Bootstrap and Spring Data JPA. Below is a screenshot:

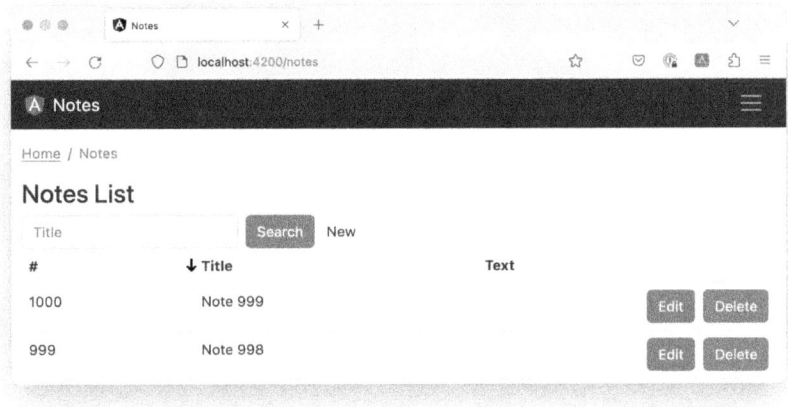

Figure 43. Notes list with sorting

Secure Your Angular + Spring Boot App with OIDC

To begin, you must create a Heroku account [https://signup.heroku.com/login]. If you already have a Heroku account, log in to it [https://id.heroku.com/login]. Once you're logged in, create a new app. I named mine bootiful-angular.

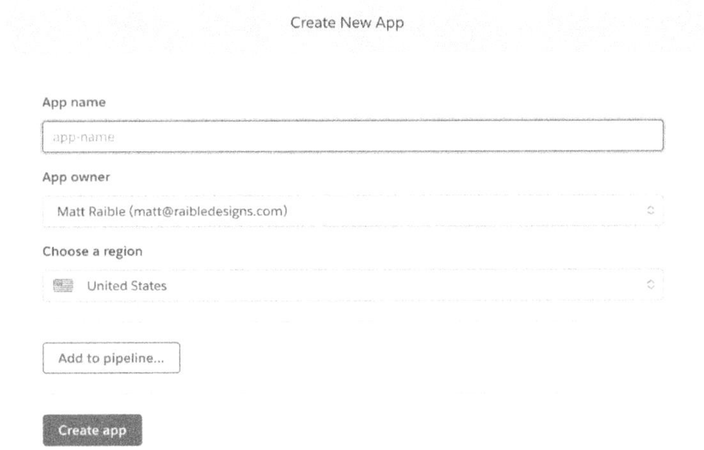

Figure 44. Create Heroku app

After creating your app, you *could* select the **Resources** tab and add the Auth0 add-on [https://elements.heroku.com/addons/auth0]. However, this will create a new Auth0 tenant for you and configure your Heroku app to use it.

It's easier to use the tenant you already configured.

Your Angular and Spring Boot apps should have their security configured to use OIDC from the last chapter. However, you'll need to configure Auth0 for both the Angular and Spring Boot apps to allow Heroku URLs.

You can run `auth0 apps list` to get the client IDs for your Auth0 apps. Then, update the URLs for your Spring Boot app, replacing `bootiful-angular` with your Heroku app's name.

```
auth0 apps update <spring-boot-client-id> \
  --callbacks http://localhost:8080/login/oauth2/code/okta,https://bootiful-
angular.herokuapp.com/login/oauth2/code/okta \
  --logout-urls http://localhost:8080,https://bootiful-angular.herokuapp.com
\
  --origins http://localhost:8080,https://bootiful-angular.herokuapp.com \
  --web-origins http://localhost:8080,https://bootiful-angular.herokuapp.com
```

Now you'll need to set the `OKTA_*` environment variables on Heroku for your Spring Boot app. You can do this by running `heroku config:set` or using the **Settings** tab in the Heroku dashboard. You can also use the following command from the `angular-deployment/notes-api` directory. If you don't have an `.okta.env` file in this directory, copy the one from the `angular-bootstrap/notes-api` directory.

```
source .okta.env
heroku config:set -a bootiful-angular \
  OKTA_OAUTH2_ISSUER=$OKTA_OAUTH2_ISSUER \
  OKTA_OAUTH2_CLIENT_ID=$OKTA_OAUTH2_CLIENT_ID \
  OKTA_OAUTH2_CLIENT_SECRET=$OKTA_OAUTH2_CLIENT_SECRET \
  OKTA_OAUTH2_AUDIENCE=$OKTA_OAUTH2_AUDIENCE
```

Go to your Heroku app's **Settings** tab and click the **Reveal Config Vars** button. The Config Vars displayed are the environment variables you just set.

Figure 45. Heroku environment variables

Deploy Your Angular + Spring Boot App to Heroku

Start your Spring Boot app by navigating to the `notes-api` directory, sourcing this file, and running `./gradlew bootRun`.

```
source .okta.env
./gradlew bootRun
```

Environment Variables in IntelliJ IDEA

If you're using IntelliJ IDEA, you can copy the contents of `.okta.env` and paste its values as environment variables. Edit the **DemoApplication** configuration, go to **Modify options > Environment variables**. Then, click the **Browse** icon on the right side of **Environment variables**.

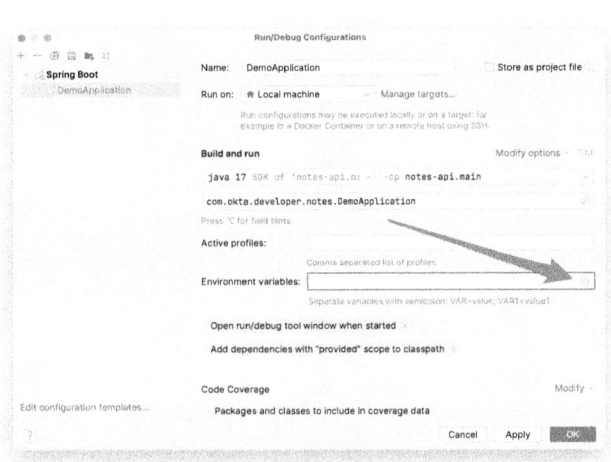

Figure 46. Edit DemoApplication Configuration

Next, click the paste icon. You'll need to delete export in the Name column. Now you can run your Spring Boot app with Auth0 from IDEA!

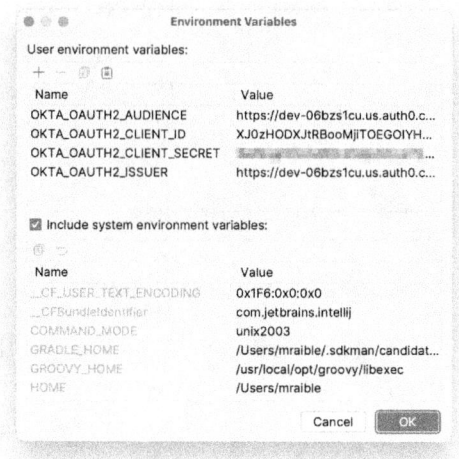

Figure 47. IntelliJ Environment Variables

Your Angular app should already be configured for OIDC authentication from the last chapter. However, if you registered a new SPA app on Auth0, you must modify auth-routing.module.ts to use the new client ID.

Listing 98. notes/src/app/auth-routing.module.ts

```
const config = {
  domain: '<your-auth0-domain>',
  clientId: '<your-client-id>',
  ...
};
```

Install your Angular app's dependencies if you haven't already, and start the application.

```
npm i
ng serve
```

Open http://localhost:4200 in your browser.

Figure 48. Angular Home

Click the **Login** button in the top right corner. You should be logged in immediately since you're already logged in to Auth0. If you want to see the full authentication flow, log out, or try it in a private window. Create a note and search for its title to make sure everything works.

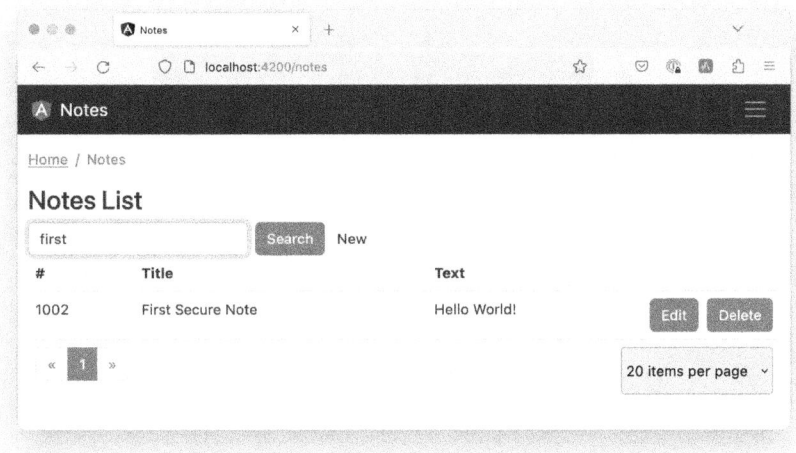

Figure 49. First note

Prepare Angular + Spring Boot for Production

You should do a couple of things to make your app ready for production.

1. Make sure you're using the latest releases

2. Configure production URLs

3. Use PostgreSQL for the production database

You're going to want to continue to develop locally—so you'll want a production mode as well as a development mode.

Update Spring Boot and Angular Dependencies

I'm the type of developer that likes to use the latest releases of open-source libraries. I do this to take advantage of new features, performance optimizations, and security fixes.

There's a Gradle Use Latest Versions Plugin [https://github.com/patrikerdes/gradle-use-latest-versions-plugin] that provides a task to update dependencies to the latest version. Configure it by adding the following to the plugins block at the top of notes-api/build.gradle.kts.

```
plugins {
    ...
    id("se.patrikerdes.use-latest-versions") version "0.2.18"
    id("com.github.ben-manes.versions") version "0.46.0"
}
```

Then run the following command in the notes-api directory to update your dependencies to the latest released versions.

```
./gradlew useLatestVersions
```

You can verify everything still works by running ./gradlew bootRun and navigating to http://localhost:8080/api/notes. You should be redirected to Auth0 to log in, then back to your app.

 If your app fails to start, you must first run source .okta.env.

For the Angular client, you can use npm-check-updates to upgrade npm dependencies.

```
npx npm-check-updates
```

At the time of this writing, npx npm-check-updates -u will upgrade auth0-angular from version 2.0.1 to 2.1.0 and TypeScript to version ~5.0.4. Since Angular 15 does not support TypeScript 5, you must downgrade it to version 4.9.5.

Listing 99. notes/package.json

```
"typescript": "~4.9.5"
```

You can also use npm update, which is included in npm since v5 [https://docs.npmjs.com/cli/v6/commands/npm-update].

Then run the following commands in the notes directory:

```
npm i
ng serve
```

Confirm you can still log in at http://localhost:4200.

Configure Production URLs

There are a few places where localhost is hard-coded:

1. notes-api/src/main/kotlin/⋯/DemoApplication.kt has http://localhost:4200

2. notes/src/app/auth-routing.module.ts has http://localhost:8080

3. notes/src/app/note/note.service.ts has http://localhost:8080

You need to change Spring Boot's code so other origins can make CORS requests, too. Angular's code needs updating, so access tokens will be sent to production URLs while API requests are sent to the correct endpoint.

Open the root directory in your favorite IDE and configure it to load notes-api as a Gradle project. Open SecurityConfiguration.kt and change the corsConfigurationSource bean so it configures the allowed origins from your Spring environment.

Listing 100. notes-api/src/main/kotlin/.../notes/SecurityConfiguration.kt

```
import org.springframework.beans.factory.annotation.Value

@Configuration
class SecurityConfiguration {

    ...

    @Value("#{ @environment['allowed.origins'] ?: {} }")
    private lateinit var allowedOrigins: List<String>

    @Bean
    fun corsConfigurationSource(): CorsConfigurationSource {
        ...
        config.allowedOrigins = allowedOrigins
        ...
    }
```

```
}
```

Define the allowed.origins property in application.properties.

Listing 101. notes-api/src/main/resources/application.properties

```
allowed.origins=http://localhost:4200
```

Angular has an environment concept [https://angular.io/guide/build] built-in. To use it, you first need to generate environments for your project.

```
ng generate environments
```

Open environment.development.ts and add an apiUrl variable for development. This file will be used when running ng serve.

Listing 102. notes/src/environments/environment.development.ts

```
export const environment = {
  production: false,
  apiUrl: 'http://localhost:8080'
};
```

Edit environment.ts to point to your production Heroku URL. Be sure to replace bootiful-angular with your app's name.

Listing 103. notes/src/environments/environment.prod.ts

```
export const environment = {
  production: true,
  apiUrl: 'https://bootiful-angular.herokuapp.com'
};
```

Update auth-routing.module.ts to use environment.apiUrl.

Listing 104. notes/src/app/auth-routing.module.ts

```
import { environment } from '../environments/environment';

const config = {
  ...
  httpInterceptor: {
    allowedList: [`${environment.apiUrl}/*`]
  },
};
```

Update `notes.service.ts` as well.

Listing 105. notes/src/app/note/note.service.ts

```
import { environment } from '../../environments/environment';
...

export class NoteService {
  ...
  api = `${environment.apiUrl}/api/notes`;
  ...

  find(filter: NoteFilter): Observable<Note[]> {
    ...

    const userNotes = `${environment.apiUrl}/user/notes`;
    ...
  }
}
```

Use PostgreSQL for the Production Database

H2 is a SQL database that works nicely for development. In production, you're going to want something a little more robust. I like PostgreSQL, so I'll use it in this example.

Similar to Angular's environments, Spring and Maven have profiles that allow you to enable different behavior for different environments.

Open `notes-api/build.gradle.kts` and change the H2 dependency so PostgreSQL is used when -Pprod is passed in.

```
if (project.hasProperty("prod")) {
    runtimeOnly("org.postgresql:postgresql")
} else {
    runtimeOnly("com.h2database:h2")
}
```

Add the following code at the bottom of the file to make the `prod` profile the default when -Pprod is included in Gradle commands.

```
val profile = if (project.hasProperty("prod")) "prod" else "dev"

tasks.bootRun {
    args("--spring.profiles.active=${profile}")
}
```

```
tasks.processResources {
    rename("application-${profile}.properties", "application.properties")
}
```

Rename `application.properties` to `application-dev.properties` and add a URL for H2 so it persists to disk, which retains data through restarts.

Listing 106. notes-api/src/main/resources/application-dev.properties

```
allowed.origins=http://localhost:4200
spring.datasource.url=jdbc:h2:file:./build/h2db/notes;DB_CLOSE_DELAY=-1
spring.jpa.hibernate.ddl-auto=update
```

Create a `notes-api/src/main/docker/postgresql.yml` so you can test your prod profile settings.

```
version: '3.8'
services:
  notes-postgresql:
    image: postgres:15.2
    environment:
      - POSTGRES_USER=notes
      - POSTGRES_PASSWORD=@-xYcoZn2
    # If you want to expose these ports outside your computer,
    # remove the "127.0.0.1:" prefix
    ports:
      - 127.0.0.1:5432:5432
```

Create an `application-prod.properties` file in the same directory as `application-dev.properties`. You'll override these properties with environment variables when you deploy to Heroku.

Listing 107. notes-api/src/main/resources/application-prod.properties

```
allowed.origins=http://localhost:4200
spring.jpa.database-platform=org.hibernate.dialect.PostgreSQLDialect
spring.jpa.hibernate.ddl-auto=update
spring.datasource.url=jdbc:postgresql://localhost:5432/notes
spring.datasource.username=notes
spring.datasource.password=@-xYcoZn2
```

You won't want to pre-populate your production database with a bunch of notes, so add a `@Profile` annotation to the top of `DataInitializer` so it only runs for the dev profile.

```
import org.springframework.context.annotation.Profile
...

@Component
@Profile("dev")
class DataInitializer(val repository: NotesRepository) : ApplicationRunner
{...}
```

To test your profiles, start PostgreSQL using Docker Compose.

```
docker compose -f src/main/docker/postgresql.yml up
```

 If you have PostgreSQL installed and running locally, you'll need to stop the process for Docker Compose to work.

In another terminal, run your Spring Boot app.

```
source .okta.env
./gradlew bootRun -Pprod
```

If it starts OK, confirm your Angular app can talk to it and get ready to deploy to production!

Deploy Spring Boot to Heroku

One of the easiest ways to interact with Heroku is with the Heroku CLI. Install it [https://devcenter.heroku.com/articles/heroku-cli] before proceeding with the instructions below.

```
brew tap heroku/brew && brew install heroku
```

Open a terminal and log in to your Heroku account.

```
heroku login
```

Heroku expects you to have one Git repo per application. However, in this particular example, multiple apps exist in the same repo. This is called a "monorepo."

Luckily, there's a heroku-buildpack-monorepo [https://elements.heroku.com/

buildpacks/lstoll/heroku-buildpack-monorepo] that allows you to deploy multiple apps from the same repo.

You should already have a Heroku app configured with Auth0 environment variables. Let's use it for hosting Spring Boot. Run `heroku apps` to see the one you created.

```
$ heroku apps
=== matt@raibledesigns.com Apps
bootiful-angular
```

You can run `heroku config -a $APP_NAME` to see your Auth0 variables. In my case, I'll be using `bootiful-angular` for $APP_NAME.

```
APP_NAME=bootiful-angular
```

Check your project into Git and associate it with the app on Heroku.

```
git init
git add .
git commit -m "Initial commit"
heroku git:remote -a $APP_NAME
```

Set the `APP_BASE` config variable to point to the `notes-api` directory. While you're there, add the monorepo and Gradle buildpacks.

```
heroku config:set APP_BASE=notes-api
heroku buildpacks:add https://github.com/lstoll/heroku-buildpack-monorepo
heroku buildpacks:add heroku/gradle
```

Attach a PostgreSQL database to your app.

```
heroku addons:create heroku-postgresql
```

Heroku will create a `DATABASE_URL` configuration variable as part of this process. It will also automatically detect Spring Boot and set variables for `SPRING_DATASOURCE_URL`, `SPRING_DATASOURCE_USERNAME`, and `SPRING_DATASOURCE_PASSWORD`. These values will override what you have in `application-prod.properties`.

By default, Heroku's Gradle support [https://devcenter.heroku.com/articles/

deploying-gradle-apps-on-heroku] runs ./gradlew build -x test. Since you want it to run ./gradlew bootJar -Pprod, you must override it by setting a GRADLE_TASK config var.

```
heroku config:set GRADLE_TASK="bootJar -Pprod"
```

Tell Heroku to use Java 17 by creating a notes-api/system.properties and specifying the Java runtime version:

```
java.runtime.version=17
```

Commit this file so it's included in your deployment.

```
git add system.properties
git commit -m "Use Java 17 on Heroku"
```

Now you're ready to deploy! Take a deep breath and witness how Heroku can deploy your Spring Boot + Kotlin app with a simple git push.

```
git push heroku main
```

When I ran this command, I received this output:

```
remote: Compressing source files... done.
remote: Building source:
remote:
remote: -----> Building on the Heroku-22 stack
remote: -----> Using buildpacks:
remote:          1. https://github.com/lstoll/heroku-buildpack-monorepo
remote:          2. heroku/gradle
remote: -----> Monorepo app detected
remote:          Copied notes-api to root of app successfully
remote: -----> Gradle app detected
remote: -----> Spring Boot detected
remote: -----> Installing OpenJDK 17... done
remote: -----> Building Gradle app...
remote: -----> executing ./gradlew bootJar -Pprod
remote:          Downloading https://services.gradle.org/distributions/gradle-
7.6.1-bin.zip
remote:
..............................................................
remote:          > Task :processResources
remote:          > Task :compileKotlin
remote:          > Task :compileJava NO-SOURCE
```

```
remote:          > Task :classes
remote:          > Task :bootJarMainClassName
remote:          > Task :bootJar
remote:
remote:          BUILD SUCCESSFUL in 1m 29s
remote:          4 actionable tasks: 4 executed
remote: -----> Discovering process types
remote:          Procfile declares types      -> (none)
remote:          Default types for buildpack -> web
remote:
remote: -----> Compressing...
remote:          Done: 112.1M
remote: -----> Launching...
remote:          Released v12
remote:          https://bootiful-angular.herokuapp.com/ deployed to Heroku
remote:
remote: Verifying deploy... done.
To https://git.heroku.com/bootiful-angular.git
 * [new branch]      main -> main
Execution time: 2 min. 17 s.
```

Run `heroku open` to open your app. You'll be redirected to Auth0 to authenticate, then back to your app. It will display a 404 error message because you have nothing mapped to /. You can fix that by adding a `HomeController` with the following code:

```
package com.okta.developer.notes

import org.springframework.security.core.annotation.AuthenticationPrincipal
import org.springframework.security.oauth2.core.oidc.user.OidcUser
import org.springframework.web.bind.annotation.GetMapping
import org.springframework.web.bind.annotation.RestController

@RestController
class HomeController {

    @GetMapping("/")
    fun hello(@AuthenticationPrincipal user: OidcUser): String {
        return "Hello, ${user.fullName}"
    }
}
```

Commit this change and run `git push heroku main` to update your app on Heroku.

Now when you access the app, it should say hello.

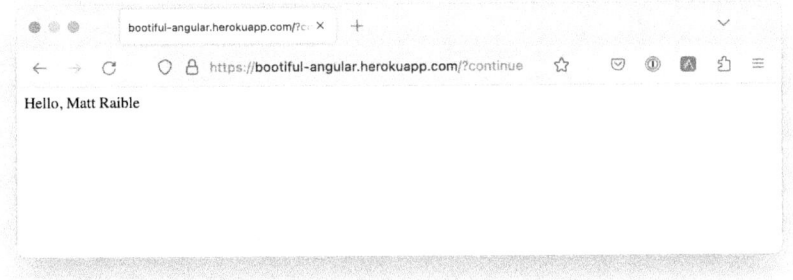

Figure 50. Hello, Matt Raible

Deploy Angular to Heroku with Secure Headers

An Angular app is composed of JavaScript, CSS, and HTML when built for production. It's extremely portable because it's just a set of static files. If you run `ng build`, the production-ready files will be created in `dist/<app-name>`. In this section, you'll learn how to use your `package.json` scripts to hook into Heroku's lifecycle and deploy them with a simple `git push`.

You'll need to create another app on Heroku for the Angular front end.

```
heroku create
```

Set the `APP_BASE` config variable and add the necessary buildpacks to the newly created app.

```
APP_NAME=<app-name-from-heroku-create>
heroku config:set APP_BASE=notes -a $APP_NAME
heroku buildpacks:add https://github.com/lstoll/heroku-buildpack-monorepo -a $APP_NAME
heroku buildpacks:add heroku/nodejs -a $APP_NAME
```

Change `notes/package.json` to have a different `start` script.

```
"start": "npx http-server-spa dist/notes index.html $PORT",
```

Add a `heroku-postbuild` script to your `package.json`:

```
"heroku-postbuild": "ng build"
```

Commit your changes, add a new Git remote for this app, and deploy!

```
git commit -am "Prepare for Heroku"
git remote add angular https://git.heroku.com/$APP_NAME.git
git push angular main
```

When it finishes deploying, you can open your Angular app with:

```
heroku open --remote angular
```

 If you experience any issues, you can run `heroku logs --remote angular` to see your app's log files.

You won't be able to log in to your app until you modify its Allowed Callback URLs on Auth0 to allow Heroku. You can do this with the Auth0 CLI:

```
auth0 apps list # to get Angular client ID
auth0 apps update <angular-client-id> \
  --callbacks http://localhost:4200/home,https://$APP_NAME.herokuapp.com/home \
  --logout-urls http://localhost:4200,https://$APP_NAME.herokuapp.com \
  --origins http://localhost:4200,https://$APP_NAME.herokuapp.com \
  --web-origins http://localhost:4200,https://$APP_NAME.herokuapp.com
```

You should be able to log in now, but you won't be able to add any notes. You need to update the allowed origins in your Spring Boot app. Run the following command to add an `ALLOWED_ORIGINS` variable in your Spring Boot app.

```
heroku config:set ALLOWED_ORIGINS=https://$APP_NAME.herokuapp.com --remote heroku
```

Now you should be able to add a note. Pat yourself on the back for a job well done!

One issue you'll experience is that you'll lose your data between restarts. This is because Hibernate is configured to update your database schema each time. Change it to simply validate your schema by overriding the `ddl-auto` value in `application-prod.properties`.

```
heroku config:set SPRING_JPA_HIBERNATE_DDL_AUTO=validate --remote heroku
```

Secure Angular Apps on Heroku

You've deployed your app to Heroku, but there are still a couple of security issues. First, if you access it using http (instead of https), it won't work. You'll get an error from the Auth0 Angular SDK in your browser's console.

The second issue is that you'll score an **F** when you test it using securityheaders.com. Heroku has a blog post on using HTTP headers to secure your site [https://blog.heroku.com/using-http-headers-to-secure-your-site] that will help you improve your score.

Create a notes/config/nginx.conf.erb file with the configuration for secure headers and redirect all HTTP requests to HTTPS.

```
daemon off;
# Heroku dynos have at least 4 cores.
worker_processes <%= ENV['NGINX_WORKERS'] || 4 %>;

events {
    use epoll;
    accept_mutex on;
    worker_connections <%= ENV['NGINX_WORKER_CONNECTIONS'] || 1024 %>;
}

http {
    gzip on;
    gzip_comp_level 2;
    gzip_min_length 512;
    gzip_proxied any; # Heroku router sends Via header

    server_tokens off;

    log_format l2met 'measure#nginx.service=$request_time
request_id=$http_x_request_id';
    access_log <%= ENV['NGINX_ACCESS_LOG_PATH'] || 'logs/nginx/access.log' %>
l2met;
    error_log <%= ENV['NGINX_ERROR_LOG_PATH'] || 'logs/nginx/error.log' %>;

    include mime.types;
    default_type application/octet-stream;
    sendfile on;

    # Must read the body in 5 seconds.
    client_body_timeout <%= ENV['NGINX_CLIENT_BODY_TIMEOUT'] || 5 %>;

    server {
```

```
listen <%= ENV["PORT"] %>;
server_name _;
keepalive_timeout 5;
client_max_body_size <%= ENV['NGINX_CLIENT_MAX_BODY_SIZE'] || 1 %>M;

root dist/notes;
index index.html;

location / {
    try_files $uri /index.html;
}

add_header Content-Security-Policy "default-src 'self'; script-src
'self' 'unsafe-inline'; style-src 'self' 'unsafe-inline'; img-src 'self'
data:; font-src 'self' data:; frame-ancestors 'none'; connect-src 'self'
https://*.auth0.com https://*.herokuapp.com; frame-src 'self'
https://*.auth0.com";
add_header Referrer-Policy "no-referrer, strict-origin-when-cross-
origin";
add_header Strict-Transport-Security "max-age=63072000;
includeSubDomains";
add_header X-Content-Type-Options nosniff;
add_header X-Frame-Options DENY;
add_header X-XSS-Protection "1; mode=block";
add_header Permissions-Policy "geolocation=(self), microphone=(),
accelerometer=(), camera=()";
    }
}
```

For config/nginx.conf.erb to be read, you have to use the Heroku NGINX buildpack [https://elements.heroku.com/buildpacks/heroku/heroku-buildpack-nginx].

Add a Procfile to the root of the notes directory.

Listing 108. notes/Procfile

```
web: bin/start-nginx-solo
```

The NGINX buildback is made for SPA applications, so you can revert the scripts section of your package.json back to what you had previously.

Listing 109. notes/package.json

```
"scripts": {
  "ng": "ng",
  "start": "ng serve",
  "build": "ng build",
  "watch": "ng build --watch --configuration development",
  "test": "ng test"
```

```
},
```

Commit your changes to Git, add the Node.js + NGINX buildpack, and redeploy your Angular app.

```
git add .
git commit -m "Configure secure headers and nginx buildpack"
heroku buildpacks:add heroku/nodejs --remote angular
heroku buildpacks:add heroku-community/nginx --remote angular
git push angular main
```

Now you'll have a security report you can be proud of!

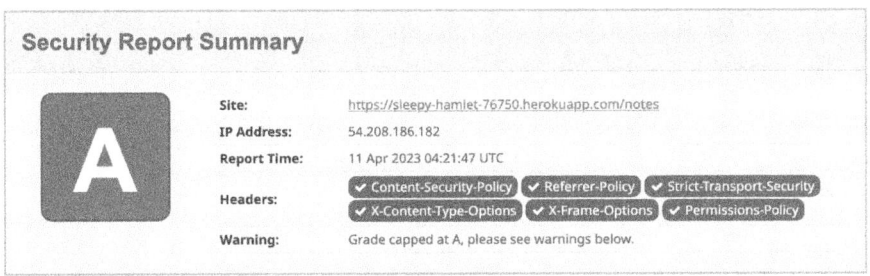

Figure 51. Security Report Summary with an A

Use `ng deploy` with Firebase, Netlify, and AWS

In Angular CLI v8.3.0, an `ng deploy` command was introduced to automate deploying to many different cloud providers. I thought it would be fun to try a few of these out and see if it's possible to optimize the headers to get the same **A** rating that you were able to get with Heroku.

Below are the current providers and packages [https://angular.io/guide/deployment] supported by this command.

Hosting provider	Package
AWS S3	@jefiozie/ngx-aws-deploy [https://www.npmjs.com/package/@jefiozie/ngx-aws-deploy]
Firebase	@angular/fire [https://npmjs.org/package/@angular/fire]

Hosting provider	Package
GitHub pages	`angular-cli-ghpages` [https://npmjs.org/package/angular-cli-ghpages]
Netlify	`@netlify-builder/deploy` [https://www.npmjs.com/package/@netlify-builder/deploy]
NPM	`ngx-deploy-npm` [https://npmjs.org/package/ngx-deploy-npm]
Vercel	`vercel init angular` [https://github.com/vercel/vercel/tree/main/examples/angular]

In the following section, I'll show you how to deploy to a few that piqued my interest (Firebase, Netlify, and AWS S3).

Angular Deployment to Firebase

Create a `firebase` branch so you can make changes without affecting the work you've done for Heroku deployments.

```
git checkout -b firebase
```

Open a browser and go to firebase.google.com. Log in to your account, go to the console, and create a new project.

Install the Firebase CLI and authenticate from your terminal:

```
npm install -g firebase-tools
firebase login --reauth
```

Run `ng add @angular/fire` in the `notes` directory, and your new project should appear in the list. When prompted for features to set up, select **ng deploy — hosting**.

```
Using package manager: npm
- Found compatible package version: @angular/fire@7.5.0.
- Package information loaded.

The package @angular/fire@7.5.0 will be installed and executed.
Would you like to proceed? Yes
```

```
- Packages successfully installed.
UPDATE package.json (1311 bytes)
- Packages installed successfully.
? What features would you like to setup? ng deploy -- hosting
Using firebase-tools version 11.25.3
? Which Firebase account would you like to use? mraible@gmail.com
- Preparing the list of your Firebase projects
? Please select a project: notes
? Please select a hosting site: https://notes-ed93c.web.app
CREATE .firebaserc (179 bytes)
UPDATE .gitignore (602 bytes)
UPDATE angular.json (3279 bytes)
UPDATE firebase.json (783 bytes)
```

Now you can run ng deploy and everything should work.

You must add the project's URL as an allowed origin in your Spring Boot app on Heroku. Copy the printed Hosting URL value and run the following command:

```
heroku config:edit --remote heroku
```

Add the new URL after your existing Heroku one, separating them with a comma. For example:

```
ALLOWED_ORIGINS='https://sleepy-hamlet-76750.herokuapp.com,https://notes-ed93c.web.app'
```

You'll also need to modify your Auth0 SPA app to add your Firebase URL as an Allowed Callback URL, Allowed Logout URL, and Allowed Web Origin. You can use the Auth0 CLI and auth0 apps open to quickly access it. For mine, I added the following:

- Allowed Callback URL: https://notes-ed93c.web.app/home
- Allowed Logout URL: https://notes-ed93c.web.app
- Allowed Web Origin: https://notes-ed93c.web.app

Open your Firebase URL in your browser, log in, and you should be able to see the note you added on Heroku.

Strong Security Headers on Firebase

If you test your new Firebase site on securityheaders.com, you'll score a **D**.

Luckily, you can configure headers [https://firebase.google.com/docs/hosting/full-config#headers] in your `firebase.json` file. Edit this file and modify the headers key like the following:

```
"headers": [
  {
    "source": "/**",
    "headers": [
      {
        "key": "Cache-Control",
        "value": "public,max-age=31536000,immutable"
      },
      {
        "key": "Content-Security-Policy",
        "value": "default-src 'self'; script-src 'self' 'unsafe-inline';
style-src 'self' 'unsafe-inline'; img-src 'self' data:; font-src 'self'
data:; frame-ancestors 'none'; connect-src 'self' https://*.auth0.com
https://*.herokuapp.com; frame-src 'self' https://*.auth0.com"
      },
      {
        "key": "Referrer-Policy",
        "value": "no-referrer, strict-origin-when-cross-origin"
      },
      {
        "key": "X-Content-Type-Options",
        "value": "nosniff"
      },
      {
        "key": "X-Frame-Options",
        "value": "DENY"
      },
      {
        "key": "X-XSS-Protection",
        "value": "1; mode=block"
      },
      {
        "key": "Permissions-Policy",
        "value": "geolocation=(self), microphone=(), accelerometer=(),
camera=()"
      }
    ]
  },
  {
    "source": "/@(ngsw-worker.js|ngsw.json)",
    "headers": [
      {
        "key": "Cache-Control",
        "value": "no-cache"
      }
    ]
  }
```

],

 You don't need to include a Strict-Transport-Security header because Firebase includes it by default.

Run ng deploy and you should get an **A** now!

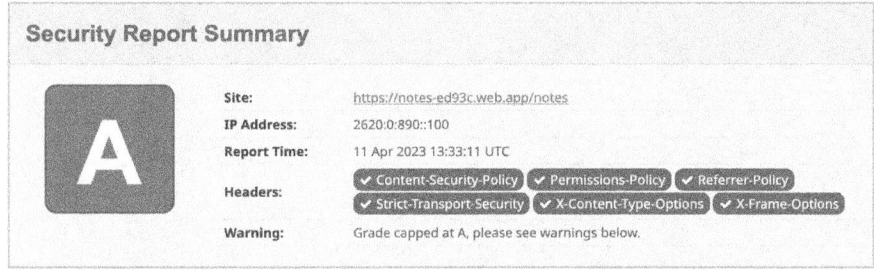

Figure 52. Firebase app score from securityheaders.com

Commit your changes to your firebase branch.

```
git add .
git commit -m "Add Firebase deployment"
```

Angular Deployment to Netlify

Netlify is a hosting provider for static sites that I've enjoyed using. They offer continuous integration, HTML forms, AWS Lambda functions, and CMS functionality.

Check out your main branch and create a new netlify one.

```
git checkout main
git checkout -b netlify
```

Before running the command to add Netlify support, you must create a Netlify account [https://app.netlify.com/signup]. Once you're signed in, create a new site by selecting **Add new site** > **Deploy Manually**. Netlify makes it easy to connect a site via Git, but since I want to demonstrate ng deploy, you'll need to create a temporary directory with an index.html file in it. I put "Hello, World" in the HTML file, then dragged the directory into my browser window.

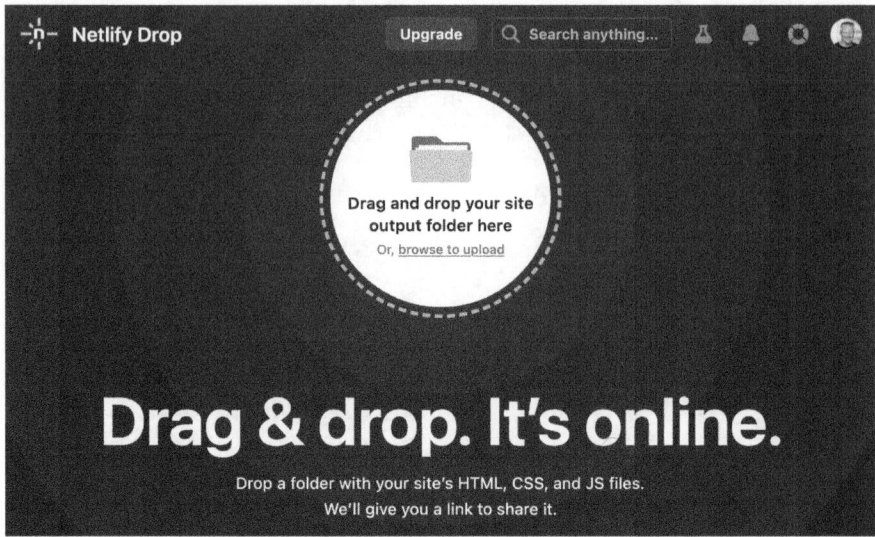

Figure 53. Netlify create site

Click on your new site > **Site Settings** to copy your **Site ID** to a text editor. You'll also need a personal access token. To create one, click on your avatar in the top right > **User settings** > **Applications** and click **New access token**. Copy the generated token to your text editor.

Run the command below to add Netlify deployment support.

```
ng add @netlify-builder/deploy
```

Copy and paste your API ID and personal access token when prompted, then run `ng deploy` to deploy your site.

Update your Spring Boot app on Heroku to allow your Netlify app URL:

```
heroku config:edit --remote heroku
```

Make sure to append the URL to your existing ones, separating them with a comma.

```
ALLOWED_ORIGINS='...,https://dapper-baklava-050b77.netlify.app'
```

You'll also need to update your Auth0 Angular app to allow the URL as a callback, login, and web origin.

If you try to log in, you'll get a Page Not Found error stemming from Auth0 trying to redirect back to your app. This happens because Netlify doesn't know your app is a SPA that manages its routes. To fix this, create a _redirects file in the notes/src directory with the following contents:

```
/*      /index.html    200
```

 You can learn more about configuring Netlify for SPAs in their documentation [https://docs.netlify.com/routing/redirects/rewrites-proxies/#history-pushstate-and-single-page-apps].

Then, modify angular.json to include this file in its assets.

```
"assets": [
  "src/_redirects",
  "src/favicon.ico",
  "src/assets"
],
```

Run ng deploy again, and you should be able to log in successfully.

Better Security Headers on Netlify

If you test your new Netlify site on securityheaders.com, you'll score a **D**. To improve your score, Netlify allows you to add custom headers [https://docs.netlify.com/routing/headers/].

Create a src/_headers file with the following contents. Note that the first line in this file indicates "all paths under /".

```
/*
  Content-Security-Policy: default-src 'self'; script-src 'self' 'unsafe-inline'; style-src 'self' 'unsafe-inline'; img-src 'self' data:; font-src 'self' data:; frame-ancestors 'none'; connect-src 'self' https://*.auth0.com https://*.herokuapp.com; frame-src 'self' https://*.auth0.com
  Referrer-Policy: no-referrer, strict-origin-when-cross-origin
  X-Content-Type-Options: nosniff
  X-Frame-Options: DENY
  X-XSS-Protection: 1; mode=block
  Permissions-Policy: geolocation=(self), microphone=(), accelerometer=(), camera=()
```

 You don't need to include a Strict-Transport-Security header because Netlify includes one by default.

Modify `angular.json` to include this file in its assets.

```
"assets": [
  "src/_headers",
  "src/_redirects",
  "src/favicon.ico",
  "src/assets"
],
```

Run `ng deploy` and you should get an **A** now!

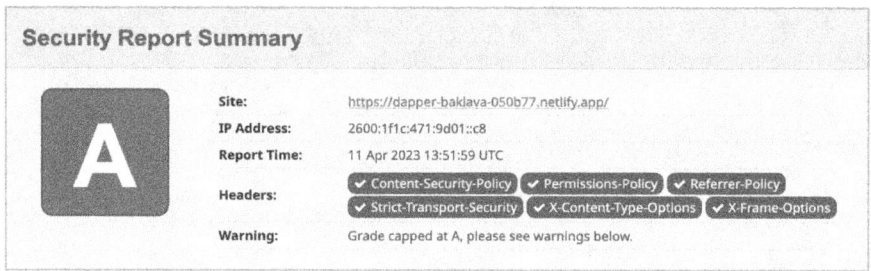

Figure 54. Netlify score from securityheaders.com

Commit your changes to the `netlify` branch.

```
git add .
git commit -am "Add Netlify deployment"
```

The Netlify schematic writes your access token to `angular.json`, which is a security risk (if you push these changes to your source control system).

```
"deploy": {
  "builder": "@netlify-builder/deploy:deploy",
  "options": {
    "outputPath": "dist/notes",
    "netlifyToken": "04b966f772XXX...",
    "siteId": "1dda959c-XXXX..."
  }
}
```

I was notified of this issue by GitGuardian [https://gitguardian.com/], which I use to monitor my repos. If you check in this change, make sure to delete the access token on Netlify.

Angular Deployment to AWS S3

Amazon Simple Storage Service (Amazon S3) is an object storage service popular for hosting static sites.

Check out your main branch and create a new aws one.

```
git checkout main
git checkout -b aws
```

Before running the command to add S3 deployment support, you'll need a few things:

- An S3 Bucket
- An AWS Region Name
- A Secret Access Key
- An Access Key ID

You'll also need to create an AWS account [https://portal.aws.amazon.com/billing/signup]. After creating an account, go to the Amazon S3 console [https://s3.console.aws.amazon.com/]. Click **Create Bucket** and give it a name you'll remember. Use the default region selected for you and click **Create Bucket**.

To create the secret access key, go to your security credentials page [https://console.aws.amazon.com/iam/home?nc2=h_m_sc#/security_credentials]. Scroll down to the **Access keys** section and select **Create access key**. Click **Show** and copy the key name and value into a text editor.

 If you have trouble creating a secret access key, see this blog post [https://aws.amazon.com/blogs/security/how-to-find-update-access-keys-password-mfa-aws-management-console/].

Add the @jefiozie/ngx-aws-deploy package to deploy to S3:

```
ng add @jefiozie/ngx-aws-deploy
```

You won't be prompted for your AWS settings because the authors have realized it's not a good idea to add secrets to angular.json.

Run ng deploy with your AWS setting to deploy your Angular app to your AWS S3 bucket.

```
NG_DEPLOY_AWS_ACCESS_KEY_ID=<KEY_ID> NG_DEPLOY_AWS_SECRET_ACCESS_KEY=<KEY> \
   NG_DEPLOY_AWS_BUCKET=<BUCKET_NAME> NG_DEPLOY_AWS_REGION=<REGION> ng deploy
```

Next, you need to configure S3 for static website hosting
[https://docs.aws.amazon.com/AmazonS3/latest/user-guide/static-website-hosting.html].
Go to your bucket > **Properties** > **Static website hosting** > **Edit**.

Type index.html for the index and error document and click **Save changes**.

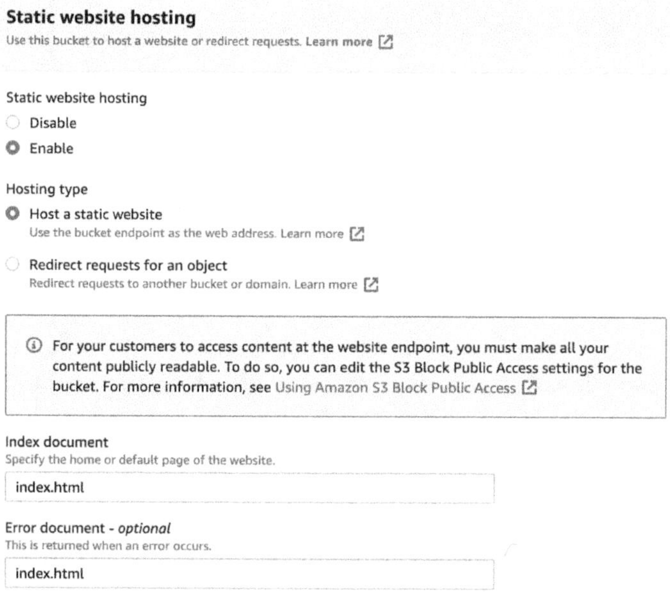

Figure 55. AWS static website

By default, Amazon S3 blocks public access to your buckets. Go to the
Permissions tab. Click the **Edit** button, clear **Block all public access**, and
click **Save changes**.

The last step you need to do to make it public is to add a bucket policy. Go to
Permissions > **Bucket Policy** > **Edit** and paste the following into the editor,
replacing <your-bucket-name> with your bucket's name.

```
{
    "Version": "2012-10-17",
    "Statement": [
        {
            "Sid": "PublicReadGetObject",
            "Effect": "Allow",
            "Principal": "*",
```

```
            "Action": ["s3:GetObject"],
            "Resource": ["arn:aws:s3:::<your-bucket-name>/*"]
        }
    ]
}
```

Click **Save changes** to continue.

At this point, you could navigate to `http://<bucket-name>.s3-website-<region-name>.amazonaws.com` in your browser, and the application will try to load. However, there's no HTTPS support. You can use CloudFront to solve this [https://aws.amazon.com/premiumsupport/knowledge-center/cloudfront-https-requests-s3/].

Open the CloudFront console [https://console.aws.amazon.com/cloudfront/] and choose **Create Distribution**. Click in the **Origin Domain Name** field, select your S3 bucket, then select **Use website endpoint**.

Set the **Viewer Protocol Policy** to `Redirect HTTP to HTTPS` and allow all HTTP methods. Under the **Response headers policy**, click **Create Policy**. Name it something you'll remember and enable all the security headers.

In the **Security headers** section, enable each header and set the values to the defaults unless specified below:

- Strict-Transport-Security: use default max-age and select `includeSubdomains`
- X-Frame-Options: `DENY`
- X-XSS-Protection: `Enabled` and select `block`
- Referrer-Policy: `strict-origin-when-cross-origin`
- Content-Security-Policy: `default-src 'self'; script-src 'self' 'unsafe-inline'; style-src 'self' 'unsafe-inline'; img-src 'self' data:; font-src 'self' data:; frame-ancestors 'none'; connect-src 'self' https://.auth0.com https://.herokuapp.com; frame-src 'self' https://*.auth0.com`

Add a Custom header for `Permissions-Policy`:

- Permissions-Policy: `geolocation=(self), microphone=(), accelerometer=(), camera=()`

Select **Origin override** if it's not selected for any headers by default. Click **Create**.

On your distribution page, refresh the **Response headers policy** options, and select the policy you just created.

Enter index.html near the bottom as the **Default Root Object**, and select **Create Distribution**. When the Last modified column changes from Deploying to today's date, navigate to the domain in your browser.

 Once you've created your distribution, it can take 20 minutes to deploy.

After your distribution is deployed, update your Spring Boot app on Heroku to allow your CloudFront URL:

```
heroku config:edit --remote heroku
```

Make sure to append the URL to your existing ones, separating them with a comma.

```
ALLOWED_ORIGINS='...,https://d1j8r5b1hr0ai8.cloudfront.net'
```

Update your Auth0 Angular app to allow the URL as a redirect, too.

Now you can authenticate to your Angular app on AWS successfully!

Awesome Security Headers with AWS CloudFront + S3

If you test your new CloudFront + S3 site on securityheaders.com, you'll get an **A**.

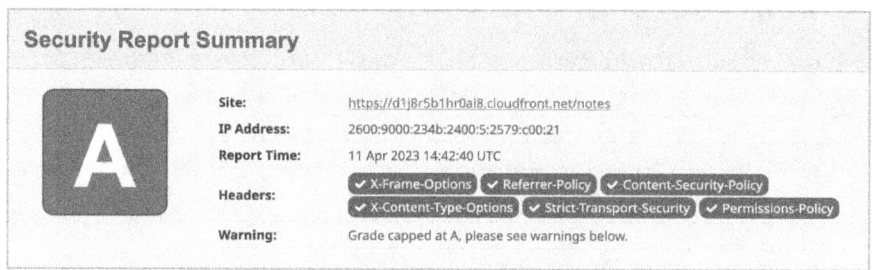

Figure 56. AWS score from securityheaders.com

Commit your changes to the aws branch.

```
git commit -am "Add AWS S3 deployment"
```

Summary

In this section, you learned how to upgrade Angular and Spring Boot to their latest versions and make them production-ready. You configured Auth0 to be aware of your production URLs and deployed both apps to Heroku. After you got them working on Heroku with PostgreSQL, you learned how to deploy the Angular app to Firebase, Netlify, and AWS.

You learned how to make your Angular app more secure with security headers, force HTTPS, and make each cloud provider SPA-aware.

 You can download the code for this book's examples from InfoQ. The `angular-deployment` directory has this chapter's completed example.

In the next section, I'll show you how to containerize and deploy your Angular and Spring Boot app with Docker. You'll learn how to combine them into a JAR and use server-side authorization code flow (the most secure OAuth 2.0 flow). As icing on the cake, I'll provide instructions for deploying to Heroku and Knative on Google Cloud!

PART
FIVE

Angular and Docker

Docker is a software platform for quickly building, testing, and deploying applications. It enables you to separate your apps from your infrastructure to deliver software faster. Creating a Docker container is relatively easy, and there are many ways to do it.

You'll learn how to use a `Dockerfile` to create an image for your Angular app and deploy it to Heroku. Then, I'll show how to combine Angular and Spring Boot into the same JAR artifact for deployment. You'll learn how to Dockerize the combined apps using Jib and Cloud Native Buildpacks. Finally, I'll show you how to deploy your Docker image to Heroku and Knative on Google Cloud.

Figure 57. Angular + Docker with a Big Hug from Spring Boot

Docker is the most popular way to build and share containers. *Dockerizing* involves packaging your app—you can also include web servers to serve up your app. This is important when containerizing an Angular app because its artifacts are just JavaScript, CSS, and HTML; the production app is static files that will need to be served up by a web server. As a bonus, you can configure the web server to send security headers that make your app more secure.

If you're following along, you should have an `angular-deployment` directory with an Angular and a Spring Boot app in it. It's a note-taking app that uses Kotlin and Spring Boot on the back end and Angular on the front end. It's secured with OpenID Connect (OIDC).

If you'd rather start from this point, download the examples for this book from InfoQ. The `angular-deployment` directory has the previous section's completed example. Copy it to `angular-docker` in your favorite code location.

If you don't have Docker installed, you can download it from docker.com [https://www.docker.com/products/docker-desktop].

Dockerize an Angular App

Create a notes/Dockerfile that uses Node.js as a base image and Nginx as a web server.

```
FROM node:18-alpine AS builder

WORKDIR /opt/web
COPY package.json package-lock.json ./
RUN npm install

ENV PATH="./node_modules/.bin:$PATH"

COPY . ./
RUN ng build

FROM nginx:1-alpine
COPY nginx.config /etc/nginx/conf.d/default.conf
COPY --from=builder /opt/web/dist/notes /usr/share/nginx/html
```

When I was trying to get everything to work, I found it handy to comment out the RUN ng build line and use the following instead:

```
RUN mkdir -p dist/notes
RUN echo "Hello, World" > dist/notes/index.html
```

This allows you to skip the lengthy Angular build process.

This will build your project and add Nginx as a web server. You must create the nginx.config file to make Nginx SPA-aware.

Listing 110. notes/nginx.config

```
server {
    listen   80;
    server_name  _;

    root /usr/share/nginx/html;
    index index.html;

    location / {
        try_files $uri /index.html;
```

```
    }
  }
```

Make sure your Docker daemon is running with docker ps. Then run the following command to build your Docker image. The ng-notes value can be whatever you want to name your image.

```
docker build -t ng-notes .
```

If it builds successfully, you'll see messages like the following:

```
writing image sha256:66c56e72ce719...
naming to docker.io/library/ng-notes
```

You can run it locally on port 4200 using the docker run command.

```
docker run -p 4200:80 ng-notes
```

Add these Docker commands as scripts to your package.json file.

```
"docker": "docker build -t ng-notes .",
"ng-notes": "docker run -p 4200:80 ng-notes"
```

The docker run command will serve up the production version of the Angular app, which should already have its back end configured to point to your Heroku app. You should have deployed your Spring Boot app to Heroku in the previous chapter.

Listing 111. notes/src/environments/environment.ts

```
export const environment = {
  production: true,
  apiUrl: 'https://<your-heroku-app>.herokuapp.com'
};
```

Since this runs the production build, you must add http://localhost:4200 as an allowed origin in your Spring Boot app on Heroku. Run the following command to make this happen.

```
heroku config:edit --app <your-heroku-app>
```

Append the URL to your existing ones, separating them with a comma.

```
ALLOWED_ORIGINS='...,http://localhost:4200'
```

 One advantage of doing this is that you can run your local Angular app against your production back end. I've found this very useful when debugging and fixing UI issues caused by production data.

Now you should be able to rebuild and run your Angular Docker container.

```
npm run docker
npm run ng-notes
```

Open your browser to `http://localhost:4200`, log in, and confirm you can add notes.

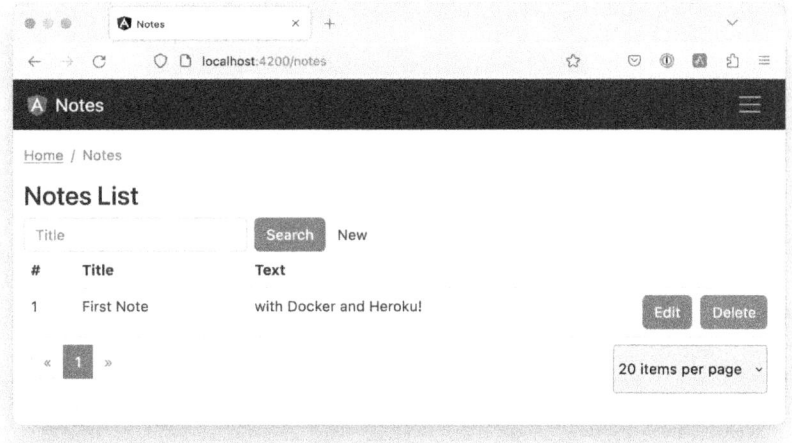

Figure 58. First Note on Heroku

Verify the data made it to Heroku by going to `https://<your-heroku-app>.herokuapp.com/api/notes`.

Deploy Angular + Docker to Heroku

Heroku has several slick features regarding Docker images [https://devcenter.heroku.com/articles/container-registry-and-runtime]. If your project has a `Dockerfile`, you can deploy your app directly using the Heroku

Container Registry.

First, ensure you're in the notes directory, then log in to the Container Registry.

```
heroku container:login
```

Then, create a new app.

```
heroku create
```

Add the angular-docker project to Git and commit it from the root directory.

```
git init
git add .
git commit -m "Initial commit"
```

Add the Git URL as a new remote named docker.

```
git remote add docker https://git.heroku.com/<your-app-name>.git
```

You'll need to update nginx.config so it reads from a $PORT environment variable if it's set; otherwise default it to 80. You can use envsubst to do this at runtime [https://michalzalecki.com/nginx-listen-on-port-docker/]. However, the default envsubst doesn't allow default variables. The good news is a8m/envsubst [https://github.com/a8m/envsubst] on GitHub does!

Replace your nginx.config with the following configuration that defaults to 80 and escapes the $uri variable so it's not replaced with a blank value.

Listing 112. notes/nginx.config

```
server {
    listen       ${PORT:-80};
    server_name  _;

    root /usr/share/nginx/html;
    index index.html;

    location / {
        try_files $$uri /index.html;
    }
}
```

You'll also need to update your `Dockerfile` so it uses the aforementioned `envsubst`.

Listing 113. notes/Dockerfile

```
FROM --platform=linux/amd64 node:18-alpine AS builder

WORKDIR /opt/web
COPY package.json package-lock.json ./
RUN npm install

ENV PATH="./node_modules/.bin:$PATH"

COPY . ./
RUN ng build

FROM --platform=linux/amd64 nginx:1-alpine
RUN apk --no-cache add curl
RUN curl -L
https://github.com/a8m/envsubst/releases/download/v1.4.2/envsubst-`uname -s`
-`uname -m` -o envsubst && \
    chmod +x envsubst && \
    mv envsubst /usr/local/bin
COPY ./nginx.config /etc/nginx/nginx.template
CMD ["/bin/sh", "-c", "envsubst < /etc/nginx/nginx.template >
/etc/nginx/conf.d/default.conf && nginx -g 'daemon off;'"]
COPY --from=builder /opt/web/dist/notes /usr/share/nginx/html
```

Then, from the `notes` directory, push your Docker image to Heroku's Container Registry.

```
heroku container:push web --remote docker
```

Once the push process has completed, release the image of your app:

```
heroku container:release web --remote docker
```

And open the app in your browser:

```
heroku open --remote docker
```

You'll need to add your app's URL to Auth0 as an allowed callback URL. Run `auth0 apps open` or log in to your Auth0 management dashboard and open the Angular app. Add the following URLs:

- Callback: https://<angular-docker-app>.herokuapp.com/home

- Logout: https://<angular-docker-app>.herokuapp.com

- Web origin: https://<angular-docker-app>.herokuapp.com

You'll need to add the new app's URL as an allowed origin in your Spring Boot app on Heroku. Run the following command to edit your Spring Boot app's configuration.

```
heroku config:edit --app <your-spring-boot-app-on-heroku>
```

Add the new URL after your existing ones, separating them with a comma. For example:

```
ALLOWED_ORIGINS='...,https://<angular-docker-app>.herokuapp.com'
```

Now you should be able to log in and see the note you created earlier.

A-Rated Security Headers for Nginx in Docker

If you test your freshly-deployed Angular app with securityheaders.com, you'll get an **F**. To solve this, modify your nginx.config to add security headers.

Listing 114. notes/nginx.config

```
server {
    listen        ${PORT:-80};
    server_name  _;

    root /usr/share/nginx/html;
    index index.html;

    location / {
        try_files $$uri /index.html;
    }

    add_header Content-Security-Policy "default-src 'self'; script-src 'self'
'unsafe-inline'; style-src 'self' 'unsafe-inline'; img-src 'self' data:;
font-src 'self' data:; frame-ancestors 'none'; connect-src 'self'
https://*.auth0.com https://*.herokuapp.com; frame-src 'self'
https://*.auth0.com";
    add_header Referrer-Policy "no-referrer, strict-origin-when-cross-
origin";
    add_header Strict-Transport-Security "max-age=63072000;
includeSubDomains";
```

```
    add_header X-Content-Type-Options nosniff;
    add_header X-Frame-Options DENY;
    add_header X-XSS-Protection "1; mode=block";
    add_header Permissions-Policy "geolocation=(self), microphone=(),
accelerometer=(), camera=()";
}
```

After updating this file, run the following commands:

```
heroku container:push web --remote docker
heroku container:release web --remote docker
```

Now you should get an **A**!

Figure 59. Nginx in Docker score from securityheaders.com

Combine Angular and Spring Boot in a Single Artifact

In the previous sections, you learned how to deploy your Angular and Spring Boot apps separately. Now I'll show you how to combine them into a single JAR for production. You'll still be able to run them independently in development, but deploying them to production will be easier because you won't have to worry about CORS (cross-origin resource sharing). I'll also convert the OAuth flows so they all happen server-side, which is more secure as the access token won't be stored in the browser.

Update Your Angular App's Authentication Mechanism

Create a new AuthService service that will communicate with your Spring Boot API for authentication logic.

Listing 115. notes/src/app/shared/auth.service.ts

```
import { Injectable } from '@angular/core';
import { Location } from '@angular/common';
import { BehaviorSubject, lastValueFrom, Observable } from 'rxjs';
import { HttpClient, HttpHeaders } from '@angular/common/http';
import { environment } from '../../environments/environment';
import { User } from './user';
import { map } from 'rxjs/operators';

const headers = new HttpHeaders().set('Accept', 'application/json');

@Injectable({
  providedIn: 'root'
})
export class AuthService {
  $authenticationState = new BehaviorSubject<boolean>(false);

  constructor(private http: HttpClient, private location: Location) {
  }

  getUser(): Observable<User> {
    return this.http.get<User>(`${environment.apiUrl}/user`, {headers})
①
      .pipe(map((response: User) => {
        if (response !== null) {
          this.$authenticationState.next(true);
        }
        return response;
      })
    );
  }

  async isAuthenticated(): Promise<boolean> {
    const user = await lastValueFrom(this.getUser());
    return user !== null;
  }

  login(): void { ②
    location.href =
`${location.origin}${this.location.prepareExternalUrl('oauth2/authoriza
tion/okta')}`;
  }

  logout(): void { ③
    this.http.post(`${environment.apiUrl}/api/logout`,
{}).subscribe((response: any) => {
      location.href = response.logoutUrl;
    });
  }
}
```

① Talk to the /user endpoint to determine authenticated status. A user object will be returned if the user is logged in.

② When the user clicks a login button, redirect them to a Spring Security endpoint to do the OAuth dance.

③ Logout using the /api/logout endpoint, which returns the Auth0 Logout API URL with required parameters.

Create a user.ts file in the same directory to hold your User model.

Listing 116. notes/src/app/shared/user.ts

```
export class User {
  sub!: number;
  fullName!: string;
}
```

Update app.component.ts to use your new AuthService in favor of Auth0's AuthService.

Listing 117. notes/src/app/app.component.ts

```
import { Component, OnInit } from '@angular/core';
import { AuthService } from './shared/auth.service';

@Component({
  selector: 'app-root',
  templateUrl: './app.component.html',
  styleUrls: ['./app.component.scss']
})
export class AppComponent implements OnInit {
  title = 'Notes';
  isAuthenticated: boolean = false;
  isCollapsed = true;

  constructor(public auth: AuthService) {
  }

  async ngOnInit() {
    this.isAuthenticated = await this.auth.isAuthenticated();
  }
}
```

Remove AuthModule and its related code from app.component.spec.ts and home.component.spec.ts. You must also add HttpClientTestingModule to their TestBed imports.

Change the buttons and link in app.component.html to reference the isAuthenticated property instead of auth.isAuthenticated$.

Listing 118. notes/src/app/app.component.html

```
<button *ngIf="!isAuthenticated" (click)="auth.login()"
        type="button" class="btn btn-outline-primary"
        id="login">Login</button>
<button *ngIf="isAuthenticated" (click)="auth.logout()"
        type="button" class="btn btn-outline-secondary"
        id="logout">Logout</button>
...
<div class="container-fluid pt-3">
  <a *ngIf="!isAuthenticated">Please log in to manage your notes.</a>
  <router-outlet *ngIf="isAuthenticated"></router-outlet>
</div>
```

Update home.component.ts to use AuthService too.

Listing 119. notes/src/app/home/home.component.ts

```
import { Component, OnInit } from '@angular/core';
import { AuthService } from '../shared/auth.service';

@Component({
  selector: 'app-home',
  templateUrl: './home.component.html',
  styleUrls: ['./home.component.scss']
})
export class HomeComponent implements OnInit {
  isAuthenticated!: boolean;

  constructor(public auth: AuthService) {
  }

  async ngOnInit() {
    this.isAuthenticated = await this.auth.isAuthenticated();
  }
}
```

Update home.component.html so it reads the isAuthenticated property.

Listing 120. notes/src/app/home/home.component.html

```
<p><a routerLink="/notes" *ngIf="isAuthenticated">View Notes</a></p>
```

Delete notes/src/app/auth-routing.module.ts.

Modify `app.module.ts` to remove the `AuthRoutingModule` import, add HomeComponent as a declaration, and import `HttpClientModule`.

Listing 121. notes/src/app/app.module.ts

```
import { NgModule } from '@angular/core';
import { BrowserModule } from '@angular/platform-browser';

import { AppRoutingModule } from './app-routing.module';
import { AppComponent } from './app.component';
import { NoteModule } from './note/note.module';
import { NgbModule } from '@ng-bootstrap/ng-bootstrap';
import { HomeComponent } from './home/home.component';
import { HttpClientModule } from '@angular/common/http';

@NgModule({
  declarations: [
    AppComponent,
    HomeComponent
  ],
  imports: [
    BrowserModule,
    AppRoutingModule,
    HttpClientModule,
    NoteModule,
    NgbModule
  ],
  providers: [],
  bootstrap: [AppComponent]
})
export class AppModule { }
```

Update `notes/src/app/note/note.routes.ts` to remove the `AuthGuard`.

Add the route for HomeComponent to `app-routing.module.ts`.

Listing 122. notes/src/app/app-routing.module.ts

```
import { HomeComponent } from './home/home.component';

const routes: Routes = [
  { path: '', redirectTo: '/home', pathMatch: 'full' },
  {
    path: 'home',
    component: HomeComponent
  }
];
```

Change both `environment.development.ts` and `environment.ts` to use a blank apiUrl.

```
  apiUrl: ''
```

Create a `proxy.conf.js` file to proxy certain requests to your Spring Boot
API on `http://localhost:8080`.

Listing 123. notes/src/proxy.conf.js

```
const PROXY_CONFIG = [
  {
    context: ['/user', '/api', '/oauth2', '/login'],
    target: 'http://localhost:8080',
    secure: false,
    logLevel: 'debug'
  }
]

module.exports = PROXY_CONFIG;
```

Add this file as a `proxyConfig` option in `angular.json`.

Listing 124. notes/angular.json

```
"serve": {
  "builder": "@angular-devkit/build-angular:dev-server",
  "configurations": {
    "production": {
      "browserTarget": "notes:build:production"
    },
    "development": {
      "browserTarget": "notes:build:development",
      "proxyConfig": "src/proxy.conf.js"
    }
  },
},
```

Remove Auth0's Angular SDK and OktaDev Schematics:

```
npm uninstall @auth0/auth0-angular @oktadev/schematics
```

At this point, your Angular app doesn't contain any Auth0-specific code for
authentication. Instead, it relies on your Spring Boot app to provide that.

In the Spring Boot app, you must adjust how the email is retrieved from the
user's profile. The easiest way to do this is to add the following property to

application-dev.properties and application-prod.properties.

```
spring.security.oauth2.client.provider.okta.user-name-
attribute=preferred_username
```

Then in DemoApplication.kt, change the AddUserToNote class to use the SecurityContextHolder to get the email.

```
class AddUserToNote {

    @HandleBeforeCreate
    fun handleCreate(note: Note) {
        val email = SecurityContextHolder.getContext().authentication.name
        note.username = email
        println("Creating note: $note")
    }
}
```

You'll need to make the same change to the email variable in UserController.kt.

```
class UserController(val repository: NotesRepository) {

    @GetMapping("/user/notes")
    fun notes(principal: Principal, title: String?, pageable: Pageable):
Page<Note> {
        val email = principal.name
        ...
    }

    ...
}
```

To log in from your Angular app, you'll need to modify the Spring Boot app on Auth0 to allow callback and logout URLs from the Angular app. Run auth0 apps open, select your Spring Boot app, and it'll open in the Auth0 dashboard. Then, add the following URLs:

- Callback: http://localhost:4200/login/oauth2/code/okta

- Logout: http://localhost:4200

Now you can run ng serve in your Angular app and source .okta.env && ./gradlew bootRun in your Spring Boot app and log in as you did before. You will not be able to log out since you haven't added the /api/logout endpoint to do so. You also won't be able to add notes because (cross-site request forgery) CSRF needs to be configured. You'll do that in the next section.

Configure Spring Boot for CSRF

To add notes, you'll need to configure Spring Boot to use CSRF. CSRF is a security measure that prevents cross-site request forgery. It works by requiring a token to be sent with every request. This token is stored in a cookie and is sent back to the server with every request. The server then checks that the token matches the one in the cookie. If it doesn't, the request is rejected.

To configure Spring Boot for CSRF, modify your `SecurityConfiguration.kt` file to add CSRF support.

Listing 125. notes-api/src/main/kotlin/.../notes/SecurityConfiguration.kt

```
...
import
org.springframework.security.web.authentication.www.BasicAuthenticationFilter
import org.springframework.security.web.csrf.CookieCsrfTokenRepository
import org.springframework.security.web.csrf.CsrfTokenRequestAttributeHandler

@Configuration
class SecurityConfiguration {

    @Bean
    fun webSecurity(http: HttpSecurity): SecurityFilterChain {
        ...

        http.csrf()

.csrfTokenRepository(CookieCsrfTokenRepository.withHttpOnlyFalse())
            .csrfTokenRequestHandler(CsrfTokenRequestAttributeHandler())

        http.addFilterAfter(CookieCsrfFilter(),
BasicAuthenticationFilter::class.java)

        ...
    }
}
```

Create a `CookieCsrfFilter.kt` file in the same package to add the CSRF token to the response.

```
package com.okta.developer.notes
```

```
import jakarta.servlet.FilterChain
import jakarta.servlet.ServletException
import jakarta.servlet.http.HttpServletRequest
import jakarta.servlet.http.HttpServletResponse
import org.springframework.security.web.csrf.CsrfToken
import org.springframework.web.filter.OncePerRequestFilter
import java.io.IOException

/**
 * Spring Security 6 doesn't set a XSRF-TOKEN cookie by default.
 * This solution is <a href="https://bit.ly/3MDwjnj">recommended</a> by
Spring Security.
 */
class CookieCsrfFilter : OncePerRequestFilter() {
    /** {@inheritDoc} */
    @Throws(ServletException::class, IOException::class)
    override fun doFilterInternal(
        request: HttpServletRequest,
        response: HttpServletResponse,
        filterChain: FilterChain
    ) {
        val csrfToken = request.getAttribute(CsrfToken::class.java.name) as
CsrfToken
        response.setHeader(csrfToken.headerName, csrfToken.token)
        filterChain.doFilter(request, response)
    }
}
```

Angular's `HttpClient` supports the client-side half of the CSRF protection. It'll read the cookie sent by Spring Boot and return it in an `X-XSRF-TOKEN` header. You can read more about this at Angular's Security docs [https://angular.io/guide/http#security-xsrf-protection].

Now you'll need to adjust your Spring Boot app to include Angular for production.

Configure Spring Boot to Include Your Angular SPA

In your Spring Boot app, you'll need to change several things. You must configure Gradle to build your Angular app when you pass in -Pprod, you must adjust its routes (so it's SPA-aware and routes all 404s to index.html), and you must modify Spring Security to allow HTML, CSS, and JavaScript to be anonymously accessed.

To begin, delete `src/main/kotlin/⋯/notes/HomeController.kt`. You'll no longer need this because your Angular app will be served up at the / path.

Next, create a `SpaWebFilter.kt` that routes all requests to `index.html`.

Listing 126. notes-api/src/main/kotlin/com/okta/developer/notes/SpaWebFilter.kt

```kotlin
package com.okta.developer.notes

import jakarta.servlet.FilterChain
import jakarta.servlet.ServletException
import jakarta.servlet.http.HttpServletRequest
import jakarta.servlet.http.HttpServletResponse
import org.springframework.web.filter.OncePerRequestFilter
import java.io.IOException

class SpaWebFilter : OncePerRequestFilter() {

    /**
     * Forwards any unmapped paths (except those containing a period) to
`index.html`.
     */
    @Throws(ServletException::class, IOException::class)
    override fun doFilterInternal(
        request: HttpServletRequest,
        response: HttpServletResponse,
        filterChain: FilterChain
    ) {
        val path = request.requestURI
        if (!path.startsWith("/api") &&
            !path.startsWith("/login") &&
            !path.startsWith("/oauth2") &&
            !path.startsWith("/user") &&
            !path.contains(".") &&
            path.matches("/(.*)".toRegex())
        ) {
            request.getRequestDispatcher("/index.html").forward(request,
response)
            return
        }
        filterChain.doFilter(request, response)
    }
}
```

Modify `SecurityConfiguration.kt` to allow anonymous access to static web files, the /user info endpoint, add the `SpaWebFilter`, and add additional security headers.

Listing 127. notes-api/src/main/kotlin/.../notes/SecurityConfiguration.kt

```kotlin
package com.okta.developer.notes

import org.springframework.beans.factory.annotation.Value
import org.springframework.context.annotation.Bean
```

```
import org.springframework.context.annotation.Configuration
import org.springframework.security.config.Customizer.withDefaults
import
org.springframework.security.config.annotation.web.builders.HttpSecurity
import
org.springframework.security.oauth2.core.DelegatingOAuth2TokenValidator
import org.springframework.security.oauth2.core.OAuth2Error
import org.springframework.security.oauth2.core.OAuth2TokenValidator
import org.springframework.security.oauth2.core.OAuth2TokenValidatorResult
import org.springframework.security.oauth2.jwt.*
import org.springframework.security.web.SecurityFilterChain
import
org.springframework.security.web.authentication.www.BasicAuthenticationFilter
import org.springframework.security.web.csrf.CookieCsrfTokenRepository
import org.springframework.security.web.csrf.CsrfTokenRequestAttributeHandler
import
org.springframework.security.web.header.writers.ReferrerPolicyHeaderWriter
import org.springframework.security.web.util.matcher.RequestMatcher
import org.springframework.web.cors.CorsConfiguration
import org.springframework.web.cors.CorsConfigurationSource
import org.springframework.web.cors.UrlBasedCorsConfigurationSource

@Configuration
class SecurityConfiguration {

    @Bean
    fun webSecurity(http: HttpSecurity): SecurityFilterChain {
        http
            .authorizeHttpRequests { authz ->
                authz.requestMatchers("/", "/index.html", "/*.js", "/*.css",
"/assets/**").permitAll()
                authz.requestMatchers("/user").permitAll()
                authz.anyRequest().authenticated()
            }
            .oauth2Login(withDefaults())
            .oauth2ResourceServer().jwt()

        http.cors()

        http.requiresChannel().requestMatchers(RequestMatcher { r ->
            r.getHeader("X-Forwarded-Proto") != null
        }).requiresSecure()

        http.csrf()

.csrfTokenRepository(CookieCsrfTokenRepository.withHttpOnlyFalse())
            .csrfTokenRequestHandler(CsrfTokenRequestAttributeHandler())

        http.addFilterAfter(SpaWebFilter(),
BasicAuthenticationFilter::class.java)
        http.addFilterAfter(CookieCsrfFilter(),
BasicAuthenticationFilter::class.java)
```

```
        http.headers { headers ->
            headers.contentSecurityPolicy("script-src 'self' 'unsafe-inline';
report-to /csp-report-endpoint/")
            headers.frameOptions { frameOptions -> frameOptions.sameOrigin()
}
            headers.referrerPolicy { referrer ->

referrer.policy(ReferrerPolicyHeaderWriter.ReferrerPolicy.STRICT_ORIGIN_WHEN_
CROSS_ORIGIN)
            }
            headers.permissionsPolicy { permissions ->
                permissions.policy("camera=(), fullscreen=(self),
geolocation=(), gyroscope=(), " +
                    "magnetometer=(), microphone=(), midi=(), payment=(),
sync-xhr=()")
            }
        }

        return http.build()
    }

    ...

}
```

See Spring Security's headers [https://docs.spring.io/spring-security/reference/features/exploits/headers.html#headers] documentation for default security headers and other options.

With Kotlin, you can mark parameters and return values as optional by adding ? to their type. Update the user() method in UserController.kt to make OidcUser optional. It will be null when the user is not authenticated; that's why this change is needed.

Listing 128. notes-api/src/main/kotlin/.../notes/UserController.kt

```
@GetMapping("/user")
fun user(@AuthenticationPrincipal user: OidcUser?): OidcUser? {
    return user
}
```

Previously, Angular handled logout. Add a LogoutController that will handle expiring the session as well as sending a logout URL back to Angular so it can sign out from Auth0.

Listing 129. notes-api/src/main/kotlin/.../notes/LogoutController.kt

```
package com.okta.developer.notes
```

```
import jakarta.servlet.http.HttpServletRequest
import org.springframework.http.HttpHeaders
import org.springframework.http.ResponseEntity
import
org.springframework.security.oauth2.client.registration.ClientRegistration
import
org.springframework.security.oauth2.client.registration.ClientRegistrationRep
ository
import org.springframework.web.bind.annotation.PostMapping
import org.springframework.web.bind.annotation.RestController

@RestController
class LogoutController(clientRegistrationRepository:
ClientRegistrationRepository) {

    val registration: ClientRegistration =
        clientRegistrationRepository.findByRegistrationId("okta")

    @PostMapping("/api/logout")
    fun logout(request: HttpServletRequest): ResponseEntity<*> {
        val issuerUri = registration.providerDetails.issuerUri
        val originUrl = request.getHeader(HttpHeaders.ORIGIN)
        val logoutUrl =

"${issuerUri}v2/logout?client_id=${registration.clientId}&returnTo=${originUr
l}"
        request.session.invalidate()
        return ResponseEntity.ok().body(java.util.Map.of("logoutUrl",
logoutUrl))
    }
}
```

You can also remove the allowed.origins property from the application-dev.properties and application-prod.properties files since Angular will proxy the request in development (eliminating the need for CORS), and there won't be cross-domain requests in production.

Add a server.port property to application-prod.properties that uses a PORT environment variable if it's set.

```
server.port=${PORT:8080}
```

Because there won't be any cross-domain requests, you can also remove the corsConfigurationSource bean, the allowedOrigins variable, and associated imports in SecurityConfiguration.kt.

Modify Gradle to Build a JAR with Angular Included

Now that your Spring Boot app is ready to serve up your Angular app, you need to modify your Gradle configuration to build your Angular app and package it in the JAR.

Start by importing `NpxTask` and adding the Node Gradle plugin.

Listing 130. notes-api/build.gradle.kts

```
import com.github.gradle.node.npm.task.NpxTask

plugins {
    ...
    id("com.github.node-gradle.node") version "3.5.1"
    ...
}
```

Then, define the location of your Angular app and configuration for the Node plugin. I added this at the bottom of the file.

```
val spa = "${projectDir}/../notes"

node {
    version.set("18")
    nodeProjectDir.set(file(spa))
}
```

Add a `buildWeb` task:

```
val buildWeb = tasks.register<NpxTask>("buildNpm") {
    dependsOn(tasks.npmInstall)
    command.set("ng")
    args.set(listOf("build"))
    inputs.dir("${spa}/src")
    inputs.dir(fileTree("${spa}/node_modules").exclude("${spa}/.cache"))
    outputs.dir("${spa}/dist")
}
```

And modify the `processResources` task to build Angular when `-Pprod` is passed in.

```
tasks.processResources {
    rename("application-${profile}.properties", "application.properties")
    if (profile == "prod") {
        dependsOn(buildWeb)
```

```
        from("${spa}/dist/notes") {
            into("static")
        }
    }
}
```

Now you should be able to combine both apps when running ./gradlew bootJar -Pprod in the notes-api directory. Once it's built, run it with the following commands and ensure everything works. You should be able to log in, create notes, and log out.

```
docker-compose -f src/main/docker/postgresql.yml up -d
source .okta.env
java -jar build/libs/*.jar
```

Congrats! You modified your Angular and Spring Boot apps to be packaged together and implemented the most secure form of OAuth 2.0 to boot!

Build a Docker Image with Jib

Since everything is done via Gradle now, you can use plugins to build a Docker container. Jib [https://github.com/GoogleContainerTools/jib] builds optimized Docker images without the need for deep mastery of Docker best practices. It reads your Gradle/Maven build files for its metadata.

To add Jib support, add its Gradle plugin.

Listing 131. notes-api/build.gradle.kts

```
plugins {
    ...
    id("com.google.cloud.tools.jib") version "3.3.1"
}
```

Then, at the end of this file, add jib configuration to specify your image name and the active Spring profile.

```
jib {
    from {
        platforms {
            platform {
                architecture = (project.properties["jibArchitecture"] ?:
"amd64").toString()
                os = "linux"
```

```
        }
      }
    }
    to {
        image = "<your-username>/bootiful-angular"
    }
    container {
        environment = mapOf("SPRING_PROFILES_ACTIVE" to profile)
    }
}
```

Run the following command to build a Docker image with Jib.

```
./gradlew jibDockerBuild -Pprod
```

 If you're building on a Mac with Apple Silicon, you'll need to specify the architecture. For example, `./gradlew jibDockerBuild -Pprod -PjibArchitecture=arm64`.

 If you want to override the image name in build.gradle.kts, you can pass in an `--image` parameter. For example, `./gradlew jibDockerBuild -Pprod --image=bootiful-ng`.

Run Your Spring Boot Docker App with Docker Compose

In theory, you should be able to run the following command to run your app.

```
docker run --publish=8080:8080 <your-username>/bootiful-angular
```

However, Spring Boot won't start because you haven't configured the Okta environment variables. You could pass them in on the command line, but specifying them in a file is easier.

You can use Docker Compose and its `env_file` option [https://docs.docker.com/compose/compose-file/#env_file] to specify environment variables.

Copy `notes-api/.okta.env` to `src/main/docker/.env`.

```
cp .okta.env src/main/docker/.env
```

Remove export at the beginning of each line. It should resemble something like the following after this change:

```
export OKTA_OAUTH2_ISSUER=https://dev-1337.us.auth0.com/
export OKTA_OAUTH2_CLIENT_ID=eEhk09l...
export OKTA_OAUTH2_CLIENT_SECRET=YIEnmp8c...
export OKTA_OAUTH2_AUDIENCE=https://dev-1337.us.auth0.com/api/v2/
```

Create a `src/main/docker/app.yml` file that configures your app to set environment variables and leverages your existing PostgreSQL container. Make sure to replace the `<your-username>` placeholder and make the image match what's in your `build.gradle.kts` file.

```
version: '3.8'
services:
  boot-app:
    image: <your-username>/bootiful-angular
    environment:
      - SPRING_DATASOURCE_URL=jdbc:postgresql://notes-postgresql:5432/notes
      - OKTA_OAUTH2_ISSUER=${OKTA_OAUTH2_ISSUER}
      - OKTA_OAUTH2_CLIENT_ID=${OKTA_OAUTH2_CLIENT_ID}
      - OKTA_OAUTH2_CLIENT_SECRET=${OKTA_OAUTH2_CLIENT_SECRET}
      - OKTA_OAUTH2_AUDIENCE=${OKTA_OAUTH2_AUDIENCE}
    ports:
      - 8080:8080
    depends_on:
      - notes-postgresql
  notes-postgresql:
    extends:
      file: postgresql.yml
      service: notes-postgresql
```

Docker Compose expects the `.env` file to be in the directory you run `docker-compose` from, so you have two choices:

1. Navigate to the `src/main/docker` directory before running `docker-compose`

2. Create a symlink to `.env` in your root directory: `ln -s src/main/docker/.env`

If you choose option #1, run:

```
cd src/main/docker
docker-compose -f app.yml up
```

Option #2 looks like this:

```
docker-compose -f src/main/docker/app.yml up
```

Deploy Your Spring Boot + Angular Container to Docker Hub

Jib makes it incredibly easy to deploy your container to Docker Hub. If you don't already have a Docker Hub account, you can create one [https://hub.docker.com/signup].

Run docker login to log into your account, then use the jib task to build **and** deploy your image.

```
./gradlew jib -Pprod
```

Isn't it cool how Jib makes it so you don't need a Dockerfile?

Run via Docker on Heroku and Knative

To deploy this container to Heroku, create a new Heroku app and add it as a Git remote.

```
heroku create
git remote add jib https://git.heroku.com/<your-new-app>.git
```

At this point, you can use the PostgreSQL add-on you already configured. If you'd like to do this, use addons:attach instead of addons:create in the following command. Since the PostgreSQL add-on is free, I will just show how to create a new one.

Add PostgreSQL to this app and configure it for Spring Boot using the following commands:

```
heroku addons:create heroku-postgresql --remote jib
heroku config:get DATABASE_URL --remote jib
heroku config:set SPRING_DATASOURCE_URL=jdbc:postgresql://<value-after-@-
from-last-command> --remote jib
heroku config:set SPRING_DATASOURCE_USERNAME=<username-value-from-last-
command> --remote jib
heroku config:set SPRING_DATASOURCE_PASSWORD=<password-value-from-last-
command> --remote jib
heroku config:set SPRING_DATASOURCE_DRIVER_CLASS_NAME=org.postgresql.Driver
```

```
--remote jib
```

 This fine-grained configuration is unnecessary when using Heroku's buildpacks to deploy your Spring Boot app. It injects scripts that set SPRING_* environment variables for you. In this case, Heroku doesn't know you're using Spring Boot since it's running in a container.

Add environment variables for Auth0 to your app.

```
source .okta.env
heroku config:set --remote jib \
  OKTA_OAUTH2_ISSUER=$OKTA_OAUTH2_ISSUER \
  OKTA_OAUTH2_CLIENT_ID=$OKTA_OAUTH2_CLIENT_ID \
  OKTA_OAUTH2_CLIENT_SECRET=$OKTA_OAUTH2_CLIENT_SECRET \
  OKTA_OAUTH2_AUDIENCE=$OKTA_OAUTH2_AUDIENCE
```

To see your database and Auth0 environment variables, run the following:

```
heroku config --remote jib
```

Run the commands below to deploy the image you deployed to Docker Hub. Replace the <⋯> placeholders with your username and app name.

```
docker tag <your-username>/bootiful-angular registry.heroku.com/<heroku-
app>/web
docker push registry.heroku.com/<heroku-app>/web
heroku container:release web --remote jib
```

For example, I used:

```
docker tag mraible/bootiful-angular registry.heroku.com/damp-thicket-
56433/web
docker push registry.heroku.com/damp-thicket-56433/web
heroku container:release web --remote jib
```

You can watch the logs to see if your container started successfully.

```
heroku logs --tail --remote jib
```

Once you've verified it has started OK, set the Hibernate configuration to only validate the schema.

```
heroku config:set SPRING_JPA_HIBERNATE_DDL_AUTO=validate --remote jib
```

You'll need to add this app's URL to Auth0 as an allowed callback URL. Run `auth0 apps open` or log in to your Auth0 management dashboard and open the Spring Boot app. Add the following URLs:

- Callback: `https://<heroku-app>.herokuapp.com/login/oauth2/code/okta`

- Logout: `https://<heroku-app>.herokuapp.com`

Now, you should be able to open your app, click the **Login** button, and authenticate!

```
heroku open --remote jib
```

If you test your Dockerfied Angular + Spring Boot app on securityheaders.com, you'll see it scores an **A**!

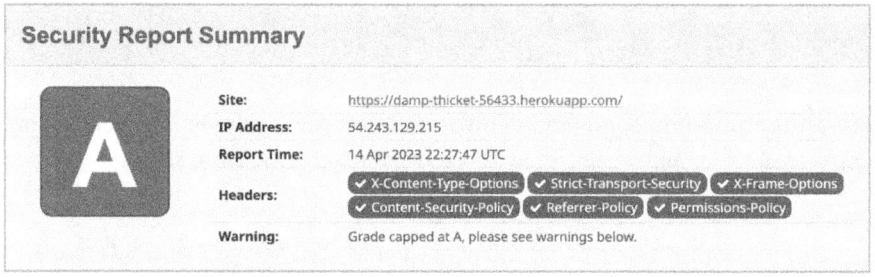

Figure 60. Security Headers with Jib

Knative with Spring Boot + Docker

Heroku is awesome, but sometimes people want more control over their infrastructure. Enter Knative. It's like Heroku in that it's a Platform as a Service (PaaS). Knative is built on top of Kubernetes, so you can install several services with a bit of YAML and `kubectl` commands.

With Heroku, when companies reach the platform's limitations, they have to go elsewhere to host their services. With Knative, you can just drop down to Kubernetes. It's Heroku for Kubernetes in a sense, but you don't have to switch to a different universe when you need additional functionality.

 Using Knative for a monolith is a bit excessive. However, I decided to include it anyway because it wasn't easy to figure out how to configure HTTPS, PostgreSQL, and Auth0. You can skip to the Cloud Native Buildpacks section if you like.

You'll need a Google Cloud account for this section. Go to cloud.google.com and click **Get started for free**.

Once you have an account, go to Google Cloud Console [https://console.cloud.google.com/] and create a new project.

Then, click on the Terminal icon in the top right to open a Cloud Shell terminal for your project.

Enable Cloud and Container APIs:

```
gcloud services enable \
  cloudapis.googleapis.com \
  container.googleapis.com \
  containerregistry.googleapis.com
```

When prompted, authorize Cloud Shell to make a GCP API call.

 This command can take a minute or two to complete.

Then, create a Kubernetes cluster called knative:

```
gcloud container clusters create knative \
  --zone=us-central1-c \
  --num-nodes=5 \
  --machine-type=n1-standard-4 \
  --enable-ip-alias \
  --scopes cloud-platform
```

You can safely ignore the warnings that result from running this command.

Next, set up a cluster administrator.

```
kubectl create clusterrolebinding cluster-admin-binding \
  --clusterrole=cluster-admin \
  --user=$(gcloud config get-value core/account)
```

Now, you should be able to install Knative!

```
kubectl apply -f \
```

```
https://github.com/knative/serving/releases/download/knative-v1.9.3/serving-
crds.yaml
```

```
kubectl apply -f \
https://github.com/knative/serving/releases/download/knative-v1.9.3/serving-
core.yaml
```

Then, install Istio:

```
kubectl apply -l knative.dev/crd-install=true -f \
https://github.com/knative/net-istio/releases/download/knative-
v1.9.2/istio.yaml
kubectl apply -f \
https://github.com/knative/net-istio/releases/download/knative-
v1.9.2/istio.yaml

while [[ $(kubectl get crd gateways.networking.istio.io -o
jsonpath='{.status.conditions[?(@.type=="Established")].status}') != 'True'
]]; do
  echo "Waiting on Istio CRDs"; sleep 1
done
```

```
kubectl apply -f \
https://github.com/knative/net-istio/releases/download/knative-v1.9.2/net-
istio.yaml
```

You'll need a domain to enable HTTPS, so set up a default domain name.

```
kubectl apply -f \
https://github.com/knative/serving/releases/download/knative-v1.9.3/serving-
default-domain.yaml
```

Install cert-manager [https://cert-manager.io/] to automatically provision and manage TLS certificates in Kubernetes.

```
kubectl apply -f \
https://github.com/jetstack/cert-manager/releases/download/v1.11.1/cert-
manager.yaml
```

```
kubectl wait --for=condition=Available -n cert-manager deployments/cert-
manager-webhook
```

Connect Knative with cert-manager:

```
kubectl apply -f \
https://github.com/knative/net-certmanager/releases/download/knative-
```

```
v1.9.3/release.yaml
```

And configure free TLS certificate issuing with Let's Encrypt [https://letsencrypt.org/].

```
kubectl apply -f - <<EOF
apiVersion: cert-manager.io/v1
kind: ClusterIssuer
metadata:
  name: letsencrypt-http01-issuer
spec:
  acme:
    privateKeySecretRef:
      name: letsencrypt
    server: https://acme-v02.api.letsencrypt.org/directory
    solvers:
    - http01:
        ingress:
          class: istio
EOF

kubectl wait --for=condition=Ready clusterissuer/letsencrypt-http01-issuer

kubectl apply -f - <<EOF
apiVersion: v1
kind: ConfigMap
metadata:
  name: config-certmanager
  namespace: knative-serving
  labels:
    networking.knative.dev/certificate-provider: cert-manager
data:
  issuerRef: |
    kind: ClusterIssuer
    name: letsencrypt-http01-issuer
EOF

kubectl apply -f - <<EOF
apiVersion: v1
kind: ConfigMap
metadata:
  name: config-network
  namespace: knative-serving
data:
  auto-tls: Enabled
EOF
```

Phew! That was a lot of kubectl and YAML, don't you think?! The good news is you're ready to deploy PostgreSQL and your Spring Boot app.

First, you must set environment variables to match your Docker and Auth0 settings.

```
# generate a random password for PostgreSQL
DB_PASSWORD=$(head -c 16 /dev/urandom | base64 -w0)
DOCKER_USERNAME=<your-dockerhub-username>
OKTA_ISSUER=<your-auth0-issuer>
OKTA_CLIENT_ID=<your-auth0-client-id>
OKTA_CLIENT_SECRET=<your-auth0-client-secret>
OKTA_AUDIENCE=<your-auth0-audience>
```

Then, run:

```
kubectl apply -f - <<EOF
apiVersion: v1
kind: PersistentVolumeClaim
metadata:
  name: pgdata
  annotations:
    volume.alpha.kubernetes.io/storage-class: default
spec:
  accessModes: [ReadWriteOnce]
  resources:
    requests:
      storage: 1Gi
---
apiVersion: apps/v1
kind: Deployment
metadata:
  name: postgres
spec:
  replicas: 1
  selector:
    matchLabels:
      service: postgres
  template:
    metadata:
      labels:
        service: postgres
    spec:
      containers:
        - name: postgres
          image: postgres:15.2
          ports:
            - containerPort: 5432
          env:
            - name: POSTGRES_DB
              value: bootiful-angular
            - name: POSTGRES_USER
              value: bootiful-angular
```

```
                - name: POSTGRES_PASSWORD
                  value: $DB_PASSWORD
            volumeMounts:
              - mountPath: /var/lib/postgresql/data
                name: pgdata
                subPath: data
        volumes:
          - name: pgdata
            persistentVolumeClaim:
              claimName: pgdata
---
apiVersion: v1
kind: Service
metadata:
  name: pgservice
spec:
  ports:
  - port: 5432
    name: pgservice
  clusterIP: None
  selector:
    service: postgres
---
apiVersion: serving.knative.dev/v1
kind: Service
metadata:
  name: bootiful-angular
spec:
  template:
    spec:
      containers:
        - image: $DOCKER_USERNAME/bootiful-angular
          env:
            - name: SPRING_DATASOURCE_URL
              value: jdbc:postgresql://pgservice:5432/bootiful-angular
            - name: SPRING_DATASOURCE_USERNAME
              value: bootiful-angular
            - name: SPRING_DATASOURCE_PASSWORD
              value: $DB_PASSWORD
            - name: OKTA_OAUTH2_ISSUER
              value: $OKTA_ISSUER
            - name: OKTA_OAUTH2_CLIENT_ID
              value: $OKTA_CLIENT_ID
            - name: OKTA_OAUTH2_CLIENT_SECRET
              value: $OKTA_CLIENT_SECRET
            - name: OKTA_OAUTH2_AUDIENCE
              value: $OKTA_AUDIENCE
EOF
```

Once the deployment is ready (use kubectl get deployments to find out), run the command below to change it so Hibernate doesn't try to recreate your schema on restart.

```
kubectl apply -f - <<EOF
apiVersion: serving.knative.dev/v1
kind: Service
metadata:
  name: bootiful-angular
spec:
  template:
    spec:
      containers:
        - image: $DOCKER_USERNAME/bootiful-angular
          env:
            - name: SPRING_DATASOURCE_URL
              value: jdbc:postgresql://pgservice:5432/bootiful-angular
            - name: SPRING_DATASOURCE_USERNAME
              value: bootiful-angular
            - name: SPRING_DATASOURCE_PASSWORD
              value: $DB_PASSWORD
            - name: OKTA_OAUTH2_ISSUER
              value: $OKTA_ISSUER
            - name: OKTA_OAUTH2_CLIENT_ID
              value: $OKTA_CLIENT_ID
            - name: OKTA_OAUTH2_CLIENT_SECRET
              value: $OKTA_CLIENT_SECRET
            - name: OKTA_OAUTH2_AUDIENCE
              value: $OKTA_AUDIENCE
            - name: SPRING_JPA_HIBERNATE_DDL_AUTO
              value: validate
EOF
```

If everything works correctly, you should be able to run the following command to get the URL of your app.

```
kubectl get ksvc
```

The result should look similar to this:

```
NAME              URL
bootiful-angular  https://bootiful-angular.default.34.72.191.176.sslip.io
```

You'll need to add this URL as an **Allowed Callback URL** and an **Allowed Logout URL** to your Spring Boot app in the Auth0 management console to log in. Access it with ease using auth0 apps open. Then, add the following URLs:

- Callback: `<app-url>/login/oauth2/code/okta`

- Logout: `<app-url>`

Then, you can sign in to your app running on Knative! Add a note or two to prove it all works.

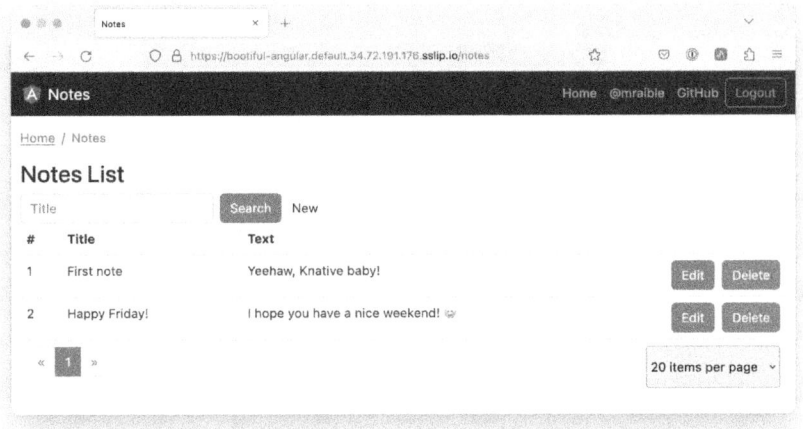

Figure 61. Angular + Spring Boot in Docker running on Knative

You will be charged for usage if you leave everything running on Google Cloud. Therefore, I recommend removing your cluster to reduce your cost.

```
gcloud container clusters delete knative --zone=us
-central1-c
```

Use Cloud Native Buildpacks to Build Docker Images

Cloud Native Buildpacks [https://buildpacks.io/] is an initiative that Pivotal and Heroku started in early 2018. It has a `pack` CLI [https://github.com/buildpacks/pack] that allows you to build Docker images using buildpacks.

Unfortunately, pack doesn't have great support for monorepos (especially in sub-directories) yet. I was unable to make it work with this app structure.

On the upside, Spring Boot's built-in support for creating Docker images works splendidly!

Easy Docker Images with Spring Boot 2.3

Spring Boot 2.3.0 [https://spring.io/blog/2020/05/15/spring-boot-2-3-0-available-now] added built-in Docker support. This support leverages Cloud Native Buildpacks, just like the pack CLI.

Spring Boot's Maven and Gradle plugins both have new commands:

- `./mvnw spring-boot:build-image`
- `./gradlew bootBuildImage`

The Paketo [https://paketo.io/] Java buildpack is used by default to create images.

By default, Spring Boot will use your `$artifactId:$version` for the image name. That is, `notes-api:0.0.1-SNAPSHOT`. You can override this with an `--imageName` parameter.

Build and run the image with the commands below.

```
./gradlew bootBuildImage --imageName <your-username>/bootiful-angular -Pprod
docker-compose -f src/main/docker/app.yml up
```

You should be able to navigate to `http://localhost:8080`, log in, and add notes.

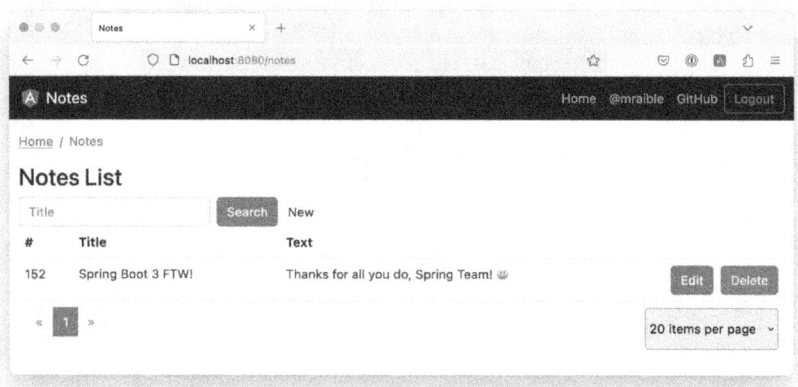

Figure 62. Spring Boot has awesome Docker support

Pretty neat, don't you think?

Summary

This final section showed you a lot of options when it comes to deploying your Angular and Spring Boot apps with Docker:

- Build Angular containers with Dockerfile
- Combine Angular and Spring Boot in a JAR
- Build Docker images with Jib
- Build Docker images with Cloud Native Buildpacks

 You can download the code for this book's examples from InfoQ. The angular-docker directory has this chapter's completed example.

As a developer, you don't want to read a book to get a baseline to start a project. The good news is JHipster [https://jhipster.tech] does everything in this book. It allows you to run your Angular and Spring Boot apps separately, use Kotlin on the server, package your apps together for production, and use Docker for distribution. If you're interested in JHipster, you're in luck: there's a JHipster Mini-Book [https://www.infoq.com/minibooks/jhipster-mini-book/]!

In the meantime, I hope you enjoy your journey developing with Angular and Spring Boot! Please contact me at @mraible { on Twitter, LinkedIn, and GitHub } if you have any questions.

Action!

I hope you've enjoyed learning how Angular can help you develop secure web applications! It's a fantastic open source project that's changed my life as a UI developer. Writing testable MVC code with TypeScript is much easier to maintain than the glob of jQuery code I used to write.

I encourage you to follow the Angular Blog [https://blog.angular.io] and @angular on Twitter.

Now that you've learned how to use Angular, Bootstrap, Spring Boot, and a bit of Kotlin, go forth and develop amazing applications!

Additional reading

If you want to learn more, here are some suggestions.

One of the most comprehensive books I've read on Angular is *ng-book: The Complete Book on Angular* [https://www.ng-book.com/2/] by Nathan Murray, Felipe Coury, Ari Lerner, and Carlos Taborda) (Fullstack.io, continuously updated).

Angular Projects [https://www.packtpub.com/product/angular-projects-second-edition/9781800205260] by Aristeidis Bampakos (Packt, July 2021) covers Angular and its ecosystem, including Angular Router, Scully, Electron, PWAs, Nx monorepo tools, NgRx, and more.

Learn how Spring Boot simplifies cloud-native application development and deployment with *Spring Boot: Up and Running* [https://www.oreilly.com/library/view/spring-boot-up/9781492076971/] by Mark Heckler (O'Reilly Media, Inc., February 2021).

I wrote *The JHipster Mini-Book* [https://www.infoq.com/minibooks/jhipster-mini-book] (InfoQ, March 2023). JHipster automates the generation of Angular + Spring Boot apps with best practices and security baked in by default!

Folks to follow

If you're on Twitter, follow these Angular experts for news, events, and howtos:

- Manfred Styer [https://twitter.com/manfredsteyer]
- Minko Gechev [https://twitter.com/mgechev]
- Tracy Lee [https://twitter.com/ladyleet]
- Alisa Duncan [https://twitter.com/alisaduncan]

For the latest happenings in the world of Spring Boot, I recommend following these fine folks:

- Josh Long [https://twitter.com/starbuxman]
- Phil Webb [https://twitter.com/phillip_webb]
- Stéphane Nicoll [https://twitter.com/snicoll]

About the author

Matt Raible is a hick from the sticks. He grew up in the backwoods of Montana with no electricity or running water. On school days, he walked a mile and a half to the bus stop. His mom and sister often led the early-morning hikes, but his BMX skills overcame this handicap later in life.

He started writing HTML, CSS, and JavaScript in the early '90s and got into Java in the late '90s. He loves the Volkswagen Bus like no one should love anything. He has a passion for skiing, mountain biking, VWs, and good beer. Matt is married to an awesome woman and amazing photographer, Trish McGinity. They love skiing, rafting, and camping with their fun-loving kids, Abbie and Jack.

Matt's blog is at raibledesigns.com. You can also find him on Twitter @mraible. Matt drives a 1966 21-Window Bus and a 1990 Vanagon Syncro.

www.ingramcontent.com/pod-product-compliance
Lightning Source LLC
Chambersburg PA
CBHW060844170526
45158CB00001B/230